The Life and Legacy of Local Workers of the MB Church in India

JAYAKER YENNAMALLA

NOTION PRESS

Published by

NOTION PRESS
Chennai, India.

ISBN: 979-8885913317

Cover design by: Kamalaker Yennamalla

In the cover picture, the late Rev. V.K. Rufus (1942-2003), a Local Worker of the MB Church in India, is preaching to villagers in the early 1960s.

To

My Beloved Parents

Devadanam and Kamalamma Yennamalla

Foreword

This book is significant. It tells a story that needs to be told more widely.

Professor Jayaker Yennamalla describes the western Christian mission in India from the perspective of the Indigenous peoples themselves. In other words, it is the story of those who responded to the Christian gospel proclaimed by western missionaries and then embraced/embodied /developed it within the context of India.

Dr. Jayaker's book, The Life and Legacy of Local Workers of the MB Church in India, focuses on one particular branch of the Christian tradition, the Mennonite Brethren. The book is a collection of biographies, telling the stories of 42 Indian Mennonite Brethren church leaders. Each biography details who these local leaders were—their upbringing, education, calling to Christian service, and contribution to the life and ministry of the Mennonite Brethren Church in India.

The story of the western Christian mission in India is

well documented, including the mission era of the Mennonite Brethren Church in the Indian states of Andhra Pradesh and Telangana. See John H. Lohrenz (1939, 1948, 1949, 1963), Abraham E. Janzen (1950, 1963, 1998), George W. Peters (1952, 1984), Paul Hiebert (1967, 1971, 1982, 2004), Peter Hamm (1967, 1970), Phyllis Martens (1971), Paul Wiebe (1988, 2004, 2010, 2013), Viola Wiebe and Marilyn Dodge (1990), and Peter Penner (1993, 1997), to name a few, some of which are viewable at http://mbhistory.org/books/. Less known are the stories of the local Indian church leaders that carried forward the witness of Mennonite Brethren churches in India following the end of the mission era. This book addresses this need.

According to Paul Wiebe (2010), the total number of North American Mennonite Brethren missionaries who served in India between 1899, when the first of them arrived, and the early 1970s, when the mission era of the MB Church in India ended with the departure of the last of the long-term missionaries, was 73; although, usually around 20 were in India at one time. Like most missionaries that came to India over the centuries, the MBs in India organized their work out of mission compounds spread across their mission territory, focusing on preaching, teaching, and constructing churches, print shops, schools, colleges, medical clinics, and hospitals.

It is true that the initiating work of the western missionaries in the beginnings of the MB Church in India was important. However, as in all other missionary contexts, none of it would have had any lasting significance had it not been for the Indigenous peoples, the local believers, who embraced/embodied/

developed the gospel message in terms that addressed the local context and took root in the states of Andhra Pradesh and Telangana.

While the western MB mission era in India ended in the early 1970s, the India MB Church has continued to grow in numbers and strength. There are now (December 2021) more than 200,000 baptized members in more than 1,031 congregations, a 10-fold increase from the time the mission era closed. Professor Jayaker's biographical collection of some of the men and women that gave leadership to the MB Church in India documents some the reasons for this remarkable growth.

Jon Isaak, Ph.D.,
Executive Secretary
Mennonite Brethren Historical Commission
Winnipeg, Manitoba, Canada
http://mbhistory.org/

Acknowledgements

I want to acknowledge all those without whom this project would not have been successful.

First and foremost, I would like to express my greatest appreciation to Dr. Jon Isaak, Executive Secretary of the MB Historical Commission Canada and USA, and other Commission members for awarding me the 'MB Project Grant 2020' to work on 'The Life and Legacy of Local Workers of the MB Church in India.' Without their support, this project would not have been completed. A particular word of thanks goes to Dr. Jon Isaak for writing the foreword.

I wish to show my appreciation to all the individuals who have helped and given valuable information about local workers who rendered their services to the emergence and growth of the MB Church in India, which helps to preserve their stories for future generations.

Besides, I would like to thank Dr. Paul Wiebe, who motivated me to work on the life stories of local workers of the Mennonite Brethren in India.

I thank Mr. G.P. Paulson, secretary of the MB Field Association Shamshabad, and its committee members, who encouraged me to write stories of local workers.

I wish to thank the Bethany MB Church Shamshabad council members and the pastor for extending their love and support.

In addition, others, including Dr. and Mrs. Jon Isaak, Mr. and Mrs. Michael J. Robinson, Dr. and Mrs. David Wiebe, Dr. and Mrs. Gordon Matties, Mr. John Nyce and Dr. Dorothy Yoder Nyce, Dr. and Mrs. Darren Dureksen and his friends, Fresno Pacific University, Fresno, Dr. and Mrs. Dalton Reimer, Dr. and Mrs. John D. Roth, Rev. Dr. Samuel Reddimalla, Dr. Hanspeter Jecker and Grantham MB Church, Ontario, Canada extended their support with the most generous hospitality to do research work smoothly in Canada, the United States of America and Switzerland, thanks to them.

I want to thank my family, wife, Samadhanam, and Children, Kamalaker and Joyson Yennamalla, for their support. Many thanks to my elder son, Kamalaker Yennamalla, for designing the cover page.

In the end, I wish to thank all my friends who appreciated my work and motivated me to continue my work.

Rev. Dr. Jayaker Yennamalla,
B.A., M. A (L)., B.D., M.Th., D.Th.,

January 27, 2022
Hyderabad, India.

Contents

Introduction

In Telangana, of erstwhile Hyderabad State, India, Dalits' socio-religious and economic conditions were severely degraded in the 1800s and into the early 1900s. In such a context, the Mennonite Brethren (MB) missionaries from the Russian Mennonite Brethren Church came to Telangana in 1889. They began their work in collaboration with the American Baptist Mission Union (ABMU). Soon, they established Mission Stations in the Nalgonda district. After ten years, in 1899,[1] the American Mennonite Brethren Mission (AMBM) came to Telangana to work alongside their Russian predecessors.

From the inception of the MB mission in India, many local workers alongside MB missionaries contributed significantly to the emergence, growth, and development

---

[1] *Foreign Missions in India, the AMBM in India 1898-1948* (Hillsoboro: Board of Foreign Missions of the Conference of the MBC North America, 1948), 17; J.H. Lohrenz, *The Mennonite Brethren Church* (Kanas: The M.B. Publishing House, 1950), 230.

of the MB Church in India. The word 'local worker(s)' is used throughout this book to refer to Christian converts who served their local communities at the grassroots level as teachers, preachers, evangelists, bible women, health workers, and social workers. In the cover picture, the late Rev. V.K. Rufus (1942-2003), a local worker of the MB Church in India, is preaching to villagers in the early 1960s.

Local workers impacted peoples' lives through their roles and contributions in evangelism, church planting, educational, literary, and medical and social services. Also, as 'agents of change,' local workers played a crucial role in bringing about socio-cultural changes. However, though local workers played a decisive role in all that took place, their contributions have not been given the attention they deserve. Hence, the author aims to highlight the life and legacy of prominent local workers of the MB Church in India.

For instance, local workers led their communities to convert to the Mennonite Brethren Church as informal agents and professionals in ministry and education. Many local workers, as indigenous agents, through their untiring efforts, led many people to Christ. Consequently, local workers throughout were critically prominent and central figures in the emergence, growth, and development of the MB Church in India.

They worked as teachers at different levels. Local workers' educational involvement has often been acknowledged and well-appreciated by all sections of the people and the government. Local workers received respect from people for their ministry as teachers. People of other faiths always identified local workers more as teachers than Christian preachers. The local people call them 'teacher(s)' for their sacrificial service.

Several stories of prominent local workers are available, which need to be highlighted and preserved for future generations. Hence, this book examines the role and contributions of prominent local workers who contributed to evangelism, church planting, educational work, literary work, healthcare, and socio-economic development. However, this book covers forty-two stories of selected prominent local workers.

In this book, the author investigates how local workers coped with daily living, met problems, completed tasks, encountered their people and people of other faiths, and adapted to life's events. The primary purpose is to highlight the life and contributions of local workers who played an important role in the emergence, growth, and development of the MB Church in India.

This book consists of two chapters and a general introduction and conclusion. The first chapter briefly describes the Mennonite Brethren Church in India. The second chapter explores the life and legacy of local workers of the MB Church in India.

Chapter 1

A Brief History of Mennonite Brethren Church in India

The Mennonite Brethren Church, which began its operations in South Telangana, India, in 1889, was born in South Russia in 1860. It is historically rooted in the Anabaptist movement of the sixteenth-century Reformation. From the beginning, evangelistic impulses have been strong among the Mennonite Brethren (MB). Edmund George Kaufman writes that even before the 1874 migration from Russia to America, the Mennonites in Russia were interested in mission work in India.[1] In 1889, Russian Mennonite Brethren Church missionaries came to Hyderabad State. In 1899, the American Mennonite Brethren Mission initiated its mission work

---

[1] Edmund George Kaufman, *The Development of the Missionary and Philanthropic Interest among the Mennonites of North America* (Indiana: The Mennonite Book Concern, 1931), 152.

in Hyderabad State. This chapter discusses the advent and growth of the Mennonite Brethren Church in India.

1.1. Historical Background of the MB Church

1.1.1. Founding of Mennonite Church

In the 1520s, in Zurich, Switzerland, Conrad Grebel, Felix Manz, George Blaurock, and others emphasised church, discipleship, peacemaking, and mission. They further rejected any connection between the church and the state, infant baptism (began to insist on adult baptism), and tithe but emphasised the free will of offerings.

On 21 January 1525, the Mennonite Church was founded in Zurich, Switzerland. Because they rejected infant baptism and the practice of believers' baptism, these believers were called 'Anabaptists,' from a Greek word meaning 're-baptisers.' Nevertheless, they preferred to be called 'brothers' and 'sisters.' Thus, in history, the early Mennonites were formerly known as 'Swiss Brethren.' Later, many became known as 'Mennonites' after their outstanding leader, Menno Simons (1496 – 1561), who joined the movement in 1536. Formerly, he was an ordained Roman Catholic priest.

Because of their beliefs and practices, the Mennonites were brutally persecuted by other Protestants and Roman Catholics. As a result, most of the early leaders of the Mennonite Church suffered martyrdom, while thousands of their followers were hounded, imprisoned, tortured, persecuted, executed, or exiled. Felix Mantz (ca. 1498 – 1527) died as the first Mennonite martyr, drowning in the Limmat River in Zurich at the hands of

Zwinglians on 5 January 1527.[2]

Mennonites usually emigrated to avoid the fierce intensity of persecution. Holland, Switzerland, and South Germany accepted invitations from William Penn to settle in Pennsylvania, America (1683), and from Catherine the Great to settle in the Russian steppes of Ukraine (1788).

1.1.2. The Formation of the Mennonite Brethren Church

On 6 January 1860,[3] MB Church was born within the Mennonite renewal in South Russia (Ukraine, at Elezabethal village) with eighteen founding members. John A. Toews comments: "The early Brethren regarded their withdrawal from the existing Mennonite Churches not as a retreat from true Mennonitism, but as a return to it."[4]

1.2. Socio-Political, Economic, and Religious Condition of Hyderabad State

Hyderabad State[5] during the nineteenth and twentieth

---

[2] Kenneth Scott Latourette, *A History of Christianity, Reformation to the Present*, A.D. 1500 – A. D. 1975, vol. 2, rev. ed. (New York: Harper & Row, Publishers, 1975), 781.

[3] Cornelius J. Dyck, *An Introduction to Mennonite History: A Popular History of the Anabaptists and the Mennonites*, 3rd ed. (Pennsylvania: Herald Press, 1993), 179, 278.

[4] John A. Toews, *A History of the Mennonite Brethren Church: Pilgrims and Pioneers* (Fresno: BCLGCMBC, 1975), 3-4.

[5] Hyderabad State, which was founded by Mir Qamruddin Chin Quilich Khan, was a multilingual princely state composed of three linguistic regions viz. Telangana (Telugu), Marathwada (Marathi) and Kanarees (Kannada). Telangana region was constituted of the nine Telugu speaking districts. They were Adilabad, Karimnagar, Warangal, Khammam, Medak, Mahabubnagar, Nalgonda and Atraf

centuries was distinctive in its socio-cultural, religious, economic, and political outlines. Politically, Hyderabad State, the largest princely state in British India, was under Muslim rule from 1310 until it merged with the Indian Union in 1948. The rulers of the Hyderabad State were known as the Nizams.

The social and economic statuses of people from lower castes were far from satisfactory. Education was backward. The social evil practices undermined the dignity and self-respect of the people in the lower castes. Dalits[6] were not admitted into schools, Temples,[7] or other social institutions. Dalits had separate gods and goddesses according to their caste. Almost every caste had their *kuladevudu* (caste god) *or kuladevatha* (caste goddess).

Beliefs in magic, witchcraft, ghosts, and other such figures were widespread. The practice of *purdah* (seclusion), female infanticide, early marriage, polygamy, forced celibacy of widows, designation of Dalit

---

Balda and Bhagat (Hyderabad). Of them, south Telangana comprises three districts - Hyderabad, Mahabubnagar and Nalgonda. Marathwada region was comprised of five Marathi speaking districts, in the north-west of the state, i.e. Aurangabad, Nanded, Osmanabad, Pharbhani and Beed. There were also three Kannada speaking districts: Gulbarga, Raichur and Bidar in the south-western part of the Hyderabad State. See V.P. Menon, *Integration of the Indian States*, Revised ed. (Hyderabad: Orient BlackSwan [1956], 2014), 283; B.S. Ramulu, *Telangana State Need of Revival* (Hyderabad: University of Social Philosophy, 2008), 28; P. Sundarayya, *Telangana People's Struggle and its Lessons* (Hyderabad: Foundation Books, 2006), 3.

[6] Dalit means 'torn part' or 'oppressed' and refers to their experiences in Indian society. The term Dalit Christian is used throughout this book to refer to Christians from Dalit backgrounds.

[7] The Hindu temples of Shiva, Rama, and certain other deities of particular importance to the upper castes.

girls/women as *dasi* (slave girl) and *devadasi* (Temple Girl), deprivation of nourishment and healthcare among women were common. The practices of *Vettichakiri* (bonded or forced labour) often exploited Dalits. Poverty, unemployment, indebtedness, and forced migration all too often came upon them.

In short, the Dalits' socio-religious and economic conditions were severely degraded in the 1800s and into the early 1900s. Into such a context, however, the American Mennonite Brethren Mission came to Telangana, of erstwhile Hyderabad State.

1.3. Advent and Growth of MB Mission in India

1.3.1. Missionary Era 1889-1958

In 1889, MB missionaries Abraham and Marian Friesen from the Russian Mennonite Brethren Church came to Hyderabad State. Russian MB Missionaries established MB Mission Station in Nalgonda and extended mission work by establishing mission stations at Suryapet (1900) and Jangaon (1902) in Nalgonda district. In 1891, the first Mennonite Brethren Church in India was organised in Nalgonda, with 178 members from the Dalit background. [8] The first local worker/preacher was Devathala Muthaiah, from the Dalit community. Besides evangelism, Missionaries established schools and hospitals on mission stations.

In 1899, missionaries of the Mennonite Brethren Church of North America came to Hyderabad State to work alongside their Russian predecessors. The first missionaries of the AMBM to India were Nikolai N. and

---

[8] Peter Penner, *Russians, North Americans and Telugus: The Mennonite Brethren Mission in India, 1885-1975* (Hillsboro: CMBS, 1997), 3.

Susie Wiebe Hiebert, Elizabeth S. Neufeld and Anna Sunderman. The two sets of missionaries (Russian and North American) carried on their mission work side by side until the outbreak of the First World War.

After the war, due to the difficulties in receiving funds from Russia, the Russian MB missionary effort was joined with the American Baptist Missionary Union. However, the American Mennonite Brethren Mission (AMBM) continued its endeavour.

The AMBM established mission stations (or which were handed over to them) in Telangana at Malakpet (1902),[9] Nagarkurnool (1904), Devarakonda (1910), Wanaparthy (1915), Shamshabad (1920), Kalwakurthy (1922), Mahabubnagar (1937), Gadwal (1937), Narayanapet (1953),[10] Janumpet (1931) (now Shadnagar, after 1940, Janumpet was no longer a separate field but, rather, only an outstation). All Mission Stations generally contained a missionaries' residence, church, school, hospital or dispensary, hostels for schoolboys and schoolgirls, and smaller buildings.

MB missionaries came to India to teach about social equality. They came as critics of the superstitions and false beliefs of the people they encountered. Dalits looked to Christianity as a source of liberation from the social bonds under which they suffered and the spiritual bonds that made them socially enslaved people. Hence, most people attracted to the mission work of the AMBM in Telangana were from Dalit backgrounds. However,

---

[9] Later, in 1913, the work transferred to Hughestown, and since 1914, the field has been known as the Hughestown mission field.

[10] Mahabubnagar and Gadwal mission fields were transferred from the Baptist mission to AMBM in 1937, while Narayanpet mission field was transferred from Charles H. Billington's India Mission to AMBM, in 1953.

many upper-caste people also converted to MB Church through local workers and missionaries' efforts.

Primary methods of mission work were personal evangelism, preaching, medical work, education, theological education, literature, publication, radio ministry, and economic development programmes. Hospitals and clinics were being built at Nagarkurnool (1912), Shamshabad (1928), Devarakonda (1929), Wanaparthy (1933), Gadwal (1947), and Jadcherla (1952).

The missionaries established schools to impart education to the poor at Malakpet (1904), Nagarkurnool (1907), Wanaparthy (1916), Devarakonda (1919), Shamshabad (1920), Mahabubnagar (1937), Gadwal (1937), Hughestown (1939), Narayanpet (1953), Kalwakurthy and Ibrahimpatnam. Boarding homes were associated with each of the mission station schools. These schools produced excellent spiritual and social leaders.

In 1920, a Bible School was opened in Nagarkurnool, which was shifted to Shamshabad and remained there until today, Mennonite Brethren Centenary Bible College.

In 1920, *Suvarthamani*, a monthly church paper in the Telugu language, and MB Printing Press started in Nagarkurnool. The Printing Press published a variety of Christian Literature in Telugu and English. Later, by 1958, the MB Radio programme and Correspondence School were initiated. MBCI aired the gospel programmes through the Far East Broadcasting Associates (FEBA) from 1958 to 1968.

Administrative Structure of MBCI, 1900-1958:

Missionary Council

⬆

The Conference of Telugu MB Church
(or MB Telugu Convention)

⬆

Field Council

⬆

Field Association (s)

⬆

Local Church

1.3.2. Post Missionary Era 1958 – 2021

On 10 October 1958,[11] MB Church in India (MBCI) was officially registered with the State Government under the banner of "The Governing Council of the Conference of the Mennonite Brethren Church of India" (GC) as a successor to AMBM to become an indigenous church.

In 1976, the properties owned and managed by the AMBM were transferred by court order to the Mennonite Brethren Property Association of India Private Limited (MBPA), incorporated in 1974.[12]

---

[11] *Brief Statement to the American Mennonite Brethren Mission Missionary Council, Shamshabad December 1958. Report of Legal Papers, Documents Pertaining To: Conference of the Mennonite Brethren Church of North America, American Mennonite Brethren Mission, Governing Council of the Conference of the Mennonite Brethren Church in India. Mahabubnagar. December 23, 1958.*

[12] The Governing Council of the Conference of the Mennonite Brethren Church of India, *Constitution of the Governing Council of the Conference of the Mennonite Brethren Church of India* (Mahabubnagar: MBCI, 2006); *Memorandum and Articles of Association of Mennonite Brethren Property Association of India Private Limited,* 1974.

The MBCI's national leadership followed the holistic mission approaches of AMBM and continued to be holistic. During this period, MBCI has witnessed the extension of its church planting to other states of India, including Andhra Pradesh, Karnataka, Maharashtra, and Delhi. In addition, several other development programmes, including MB Development Organization (1980), Church Extension Workers (CEW), Junior College (1989), etc., were initiated.

On the other hand, MB mission experienced a decline during the post-missionary. Several programmes of the MBCI, including MB clinics, hospitals, village schools, High schools (several), etc., were defunct. Furthermore, other activities, such as Interfaith and Urban Ministries, Literature Ministry, Radio Ministry, Christian Education, etc., were discontinued during the post-missionary era.

Administrative Structure of MBCI, 1958-2021:

The Governing Council of the Conference of the
MB Church of India (GC)

MB Board of Evangelism and Church Ministries

Field Association (s)

↑

Local Church

1.4. The Challenges to the MB Church in India

Today, the church must deal with particular challenges: The persistence of the caste system, spiritual lukewarmness, love of power, misuse of the priesthood of all believers, lack of unity, nepotism, lack of able leadership, dowry system, and poverty.[13] Dependency is another challenge. Since its inception, MB Church has depended on MB Mission (North America) funding for several ministry activities, which is limited. Indian MB Church should develop an inland, autonomous, self-supported, and self-involved service method rather than MB Mission.

To sum up, MBCI, through its evangelism, educational institutions, medical and relief assistance, and socio-economic development programmes, contributed substantially to building up the nation in various ways. MB mission schools played a more significant role in raising great leaders for Andhra Pradesh and Telangana states. MBCI is the largest conference among the Indian Mennonites and the Global Mennonite Brethren family. In December 2021, MBCI had more than two lakh members in the 1031 congregation.

The ensuing chapter highlights the life and legacy of local workers of the MB Church in India.

---

[13] Jayaker Yennamalla, "Mennonite Brethren Mission in India Then and Now: Thee Need for Ongoing Renewal," (paper presented at International Colloquium on 'Renewal Movements and Anabaptist History,' Bienenberg, Liestal, Switzerland, 28 March 2019).

Chapter 2

The Life and Legacy of Local Workers of the MB Church in India

Since the inception of the Mennonite Brethren Mission in the Telangana region, India, local workers as indigenous agents have led and served their local communities at the grassroots level as preacher-evangelists, healthcare workers, teachers, and social workers. Their tireless efforts brought about social change. All sections of the people appreciated their role and contribution well. They received respect from people for their ministry as teachers. People, irrespective of caste, creed, and status, always identified local workers as agents of change more than Christian preachers. This chapter examines the role and contributions of prominent local workers to the emergence and growth of the MB church in India.

2.1.

The Life and Legacy of
Rev. Abel P. Ballem (1907–1999)

Abel P. Ballem "B.P. Abel" – preacher and evangelist, hails from Shivannagudem village, Devarakonda, Nalgonda district. He was born in March 1907 in Kothapalli village near Nalgonda, his mother's native village. His family belonged to the low caste community.

On 7 May 1931, Abel married Shanthamma, daughter of Y.V. Papamma, at Devarakonda. Rev. R. Samson Rangaiah solemnised their marriage. They were blessed with eight daughters and two sons. On 17 June 1999, Abel went to be with the Lord at 93.

Abel studied at MB Mission School Malakpet/Isamia Bazar (1914-15, 1916-17) and the MB Mission Middle School, Shamshabad, from 1919-1926. After schooling, he had a theological course at MB Bible school in Nagarkurnool and Shamshabad from 1927 to 1929. While studying in Shamshabad, Abel accepted the Lord Jesus as his personal Saviour and Lord. He was baptised on 18 April 1922.

For over sixty years, Abel preached the good news of Jesus Christ to the poor and subaltern people. Most of his believers were from the Dalit background. In the 1900s, Indian society witnessed high illiteracy, and caste discrimination was rampant. The level of education among the low castes was low. Before the advent of Christian missions, Dalit children had experienced consistent denial of access to education. Almost all of them remained illiterate.

Abel started village schools in several villages like Sarampet, Nallaballi, and Samsthan Narayanpur and imparted education to Dalit children. Many poor Dalits flocked to learn about the new message of salvation, equality in God's sight, and peace through his ministry. Abel and his wife Shanthamma travelled from village to village, preaching the message that 'Jesus Saves.' He always encouraged young people to choose pastoral ministry.

From 1941 to 1947, Abel served as the headmaster of MB Primary School, Hughestown. He served as the Assistant Pastor (1956-1958) and the Pastor (1963-1996) of the Bethel MB Church, Hughestown, Musheerabad, Secunderabad. During his tenure, Abel played a significant role in establishing satellite churches in Hyderabad and suburban – at Nayapool, Sanathnagar, Bandlaguda Nagole, etc.

"His sermons consistently reflected a theology of peace and kingdom citizenship with Jesus Christ as King… He was not an academic scholar, yet his sermons were clear, thoroughly biblical, uncompromising, challenging, and fiery," says Vidya Narimalla.[1] Throughout his life, he lived a simple and exemplary life. He used a bicycle to visit people and used public transportation for longer distances. Abel lived a life of integrity, respected by both believers and unbelievers.

---

[1] Vidya Narimalla, "Abel P. Ballem (1907–1999): Invited into God's Story," *Profiles of Mennonite Faith* No. 51 (Winter 2012).

2.2.

The Life and Legacy of
Rev. P.V. Abraham (1901 - 1991)

braham P.V. – village evangelist, church planter, and pastor, was born in 1901 in Sokkanna Pally village, [2] near Veldanda, Kalwakurthy, Nagarkurnool district, Telangana State. He married Rahelamma, and after her death, he married Lalithamma, Rahelamma's sister. God blessed them with three children: Joseph, Danamma, and David. On 16 November 1991, Abraham died in the MB Church, Irvin.

In Chedurupally village, Pastor John Papaiah imparted education to Abraham. In addition, he learned about Jesus Christ. Accordingly, he accepted the Lord Jesus as his saviour. In 1922, Rev. Balzar, MB missionary, and G. Gamaliyelu *panthulu* baptised him in a tank at Brahmanapally village, Madgula Mandal.

He had a three-year Bible School training from 1930 to 1933 at Shamshabad. After seminary education, he began his ministry in Chedurupally village. Initially, he worked among the sheep-grazing *Golla (Yadavas)* caste people. Several times, the people of the shepherd caste community persecuted him. On some day, *Golla* caste people beat him severely. Many other villagers suggested filing a case against them to *Police Patel* (village Police Officer). However, *panthulu* said that they did not know

---

[2] P.V. Abraham, "Sevaku devuni yokka pilupu" [God's call to ministry], Manuscript, 18 April 1988, Irvin, Kalwakurthy; Interview with P.A. David, second son of Rev. P.V. Abraham, Chandrayan Gutta, Hyderabad, December 20, 2020.

what they were doing. He forgave them. Through his ministry, Jakkula Lingaiah embraced Christianity from a shepherd caste community. With the help of J.J. Dick, Abraham built a church in Chedurpally.

Abraham evangelised several villages, including Lingareddy Pally, Gundala, Badoni Pally, Jillella, Irvin, and Madgula. He established five MB Congregations in Chedurpally, Lingareddy Pally, Jillella, Irvin, and Madgula. Also, Abraham became instrumental in constructing churches in Chedurpally and Irvin villages. He baptised hundreds of people in those villages.

Rev. Hiebert transferred him from Chedurupally to Thandra and Kotra villages, where he worked for three years. His wife, Rahelamma, died there. Hence, he moved to Irvin village. Later, he married Lalithamma, Rahelamma's sister. After their marriage, they went for a regular seminary course from 1947 to 1949. After the seminary education, they lived in Chedurupally, then moved to Irvin and remained there until he went to be with the heavenly father. In the 1980s, he received ₹ 70 per month as an honorarium from the MB Conference.

He was nicknamed '*Yeddu Abraham Panthulu*' (Ox Abraham Panthulu) because his means of transportation was an ox. He used to ride an ox to visit villages and preach the good news of Jesus Christ. He chooses market places for evangelism. Abraham was also an *Ayurvedic* doctor. He was known for his 'medical ministry.' He saved many people from deadly diseases. He and his wife, Lalithamma, worked to empower the poor and needy.

2.3.

The Life and Legacy of
Rev. G.C. Anandam (1968-2016)

Anandam G.C. – Preacher, church planter, writer, and editor was born on 26 January 1968[3] in Wanaparthy, Telangana State. His parents, Chandriah and Balamma Gandham. His father worked as an office attendant at Indian MB School Wanaparthy. Chandraiah was transferred to MBC high school Mahabubnagar and remained so until retirement.

Anandam married Susheela on 20 May 1993, daughter of Mr. and Mrs. K. Moshe of Mahabubnagar, in Olive MB Church, Wanaparthy. Rev P.A. Paul solemnised their marriage. They were blessed with three children: Emmanuel, John Bunyan, and a daughter, Nissi Krupa. Their elder son, G.A. Emmanuel, is pursuing a Bachelor of Divinity degree at MBC Bible College, Shamshabad, from the Senate of Serampore.

Anandam had his schooling from the first to the tenth standard in MB High School Wanaparthy, from 1973 to 1983. He studied intermediate (+2) at Government Junior College, Wanaparthy, from 1983 to 1985. Then,

---

[3] Interview with G.A. Emmanuel, eldest son of Rev. G.C. Anandam, Mahabubnagar, 20 February 2021; G.C. Anandam, "Sakshyam" [Testimony], a printed document, Nagarukurnool, n.d. *MB Mission Centenary Celebrations Nagarkurnool (1904-2004). Souvenir* (Nagarkurnool: MB Church Nagarkurnool, 2004); "Life History of Rev. G.C. Anandam." in *Mennonite Brethren Theological Graduates with Their Life History and Literary Contributions*, compiled by D.N. Purushotham (Hyderabad: G.J. Douglas, 2012), 462.

he studied a one-year Certificate in Theology (C.Th) course at MB Bethany Bible Institute, Shamshabad, from 1985 to 1986. He completed a Bachelor of Theology at the South India Biblical Seminary, Anandgiri, Bangarpet, Karnataka, from 1988 to 1991. He also studied Bachelor of Divinity at MB Bible College, Shamshabad (2007-2010).

Anandam was an evangelist, preacher, and church planter with over 21 years of ministry experience in the MB Conference. On 1 December 1986, he was appointed as a Christian Education Worker in the MB Christian Education (GC), Nagarkurnool, and remained for two years. After returning from Bangerpet, he worked as a Christian Education Worker from 1991 to 1993. In 1993, he served as associate pastor in Zion MB Church Kothakota, Wanaparthy district. On 1 May 1994, he was appointed a Pastor of the MB Church, Mission Compound, Nagarkurnool. Soon, in the same year, he became chairman of the Church and remained so until 2007. From 2010 to 2016, he served as Pastor and Chairman of the Eschol MB church, Devarakadra, a Calvary MB Church satellite church, Mahabubnagar.

Anandam was best known for evangelism and church planting in the Indian MB Conference. While in Nagarkurnool, he travelled to nearby villages on a bicycle and preached the gospel daily. Particularly, through his evangelism, many people in Indrakal village embraced Christianity, irrespective of caste and creed. He received a Commissioning in 1997 and an ordination in 2000 by the MB Conference (GC). Moreover, as a Christian Marriage Registrar, he solemnised many Christian marriages.

He also contributed to the field of Christian literature. Anandam wrote several articles in *Suvarthamani*, an official magazine of the MB Church of India. In July 1999, he started a monthly magazine called *Anudina Jivaharam* ('Daily Bread of Life'), which catered to the spiritual needs of pastors, evangelists, lay leaders, and believers immensely.

After his death, his wife, Susheela Anandam, is in charge of the Prayer Tower of Calvary Mennonite Brethren Church, Mahabubnagar, praying for the needy and sick. She is encouraging people to expand His Kingdom.

2.4.

The Life and Legacy of
Rev. C.J. Asheervadam (1910-1993)

Asheervadam C.J. - pastor, evangelist, peacemaker, and administrator was born to C. Jacob (Yakobu) and Marthamma on 15 December 1910,[4] in Veldanda village, Kalwakurthy, Nagarkurnool district. His parents' native place was Sinaarikatta village, Podili Taluk, Nellore district, Andhra Pradesh. In the early 1900s, they left their native place for Nagarkurnool. Daniel F. Bergthold appointed them as village preachers at Veldandda village, where C.J. Asheervadam was born.

Asheervadam married Rajamma, daughter of Anthaiah and Esther, on August 2, 1938. Rajamma studied up to the seventh class. She worked as a teacher. They both had completed a Bible Training course in 1943. Later, they served as preachers in Papagal village from 1944 to 1947. They were blessed with a son, C. Yakobu. Unfortunately, Rajamma received a heavenly call on 15 August 1947. In the same year, Asheervadam married Harriet, daughter of Moshe, in Thummenpeta village. C. Yakobu, C. David, C. Paul, Priscilla, Santhoshamma, and Navamani were born to Asheervadam.

In 1950, during the period of Casper missionary, Asheervadam and Rajamma were appointed as preachers in Raamaaji Palle village. Asheervadam also evangelised in Lingala, Vennecherla, Thudukurthy, Thimmajipeta,

---

[4] Interview with C.A. David, Secretary MB Church, Achampeta, 23 November 2020.

Ippakunta, Achampeta, and other villages. He also contributed to building churches in these villages. During the period of Rev. A.A. Unruh, Asheervadam served as Circuit Leader of Lingala.

In 1967,[5] Asheervadam was ordained. He served as Chairman of the Evangelism Committee (GC). He worked with MB pastors and evangelists in Hyderabad, Shadnagar, Shamshabd, Narayanpeta, Kollapuram, and Mahabubnagar. He always encouraged his co-partners to extend MB Church in Telangana. He toured almost the entire MB mission area in Telangana.

He served as chairman, secretary, and treasurer of MB Field Association Nagarkurnool for several years. He also served as a member of the Governing Council of the Conference of the MB Church of India (GC) and chairman of the MB Board of Evangelism and Church Ministries. He also served as chairman of the MBC Education Committee and Property Committee, Nagakurnool. He solemnised hundreds of marriages.

On 9 May 1993, Asheervadam slept in the Lord. Due to his holistic mission approach, Christians and people of other faiths knew him as '*Raamaaji Palli Panthulu*.' He worked to empower the socio-economic and marginalised communities throughout his ministry. Asheervadam showed Christ's love through word and deed until his last breath.

---

[5] C.A. David, "A Brief Introduction of Late. Rev. C.J. Asheervadam," *MB Mission Centenary Celebrations Nagarkurnool (1904-2004). Souvenir* (Nagarkurnool: MB Church Nagarkurnool, 2004).

2.5.

The Life and Legacy of
Rev. Benjamin Kore (1941-2011)

Benjamin Kore "K.R. Benjamin" – evangelist, church planter, and paramedical worker, was born in 1941 to Pastor Rathnam and Susanamma Kore of Debbadagudem village, Kandukur, Ranga Reddy district, Telangana State. His parents were senior village pastors in Debbadagudem village from Shamshabad Mennonite Brethren (MB) Field. Benjamin married Marjiana. They were blessed with three sons and one daughter.[6]

He had his schooling at MB High School Shamshabad. Benjamin also completed a Bachelor of Divinity course at Andhra Christian Theological College, Secunderabad, from the Senate of Serampore College (University) in 1987.

After schooling, he worked as a 'Health Inspector' in the Government Malaria Department from 1958 to 1960. However, in 1960, Benjamin left the Government job to join the MB Medical Centre Jadcherla as an x-ray and dental technician. He continued this job for fourteen years until 1974.

In 1974, he went to the United States of America to pursue a two-year theological course at Winkler Bible College from 1974 to 1976. On his return to India in 1976, he left the MB Medical Centre and joined the Bible Centred Ministries International (BCM). He served as Director of BCM Andhra Pradesh from 1976 to 2008.

---

[6] Interview with K.B. Timothy, eldest son of Rev. K.R. Benjamin, on the phone, 19 May 2021.

During his tenure, he reached thousands of children and youth with the gospel of Jesus Christ. In 2008, Benjamin left the BCM and continued his ministry until he died in 2011.

Though he served as Director of BCM, he never gave up his focus on MB's mission. He contributed generously to the development of MB Church in India. Benjamin built several MB church buildings in the Kalwakurthy area – Peddapur, Gundala, and a church building at Mudireddy Pally, near Jadcherla. However, in the road extension (National Highway No. 44), this building has disappeared today. He also supported MB Churches at Debbadagudem, Gafoornagar, Shabad, and Papireddy Gudem villages of the Shamshabad Field.

He was known for his children and youth ministry among MB Churches in India. His goal was to feed the spirit and soul through the teaching of the Bible. In addition, it provides quality programmes and activities that instill biblical principles and values into a child's whole life. Because Children are a blessing from the Lord, with these blessings come responsibilities. Parents are responsible for helping children grow physically, intellectually, emotionally, and spiritually. At the same time, Churches are responsible for children, providing an environment in which they are safe and encouraged to develop their spiritual life.

He was a God's Servant with multi-talents. His ministry was striving to meet the spiritual needs of children, youth, and adults. He regularly visited MB High Schools and MB boarding hostels in Telangana – Shamshabad, Mahabubnagar, and Narayanpet and taught students Bible stories.

Benjamin also conducted Youth Camps and Retreats among MB Churches. To reach young minds with the gospel of Jesus Christ, he introduced modern tools like visual aids – videos, slide shows, and movies, which significantly impacted young minds.

Thus, he played a significant role in reaching children, young men, and women for Christ and disciple them in God's Word. Accordingly, many children and youth decided to follow Christ. They became potential leaders and faithful servants of God in the MB Conference.

2.6.

The Life and Legacy of
Benjamin and Sharamma Perumalla

Benjamin and Sharamma Perumalla were village preachers for about 60 years in the American Mennonite Brethren Mission (AMBM), South Telangana, of erstwhile Hyderabad State. Benjamin's parents are Balaiah and Pulamma Perumalla.

On 6 May 1929, Benjamin married Sharamma, daughter of Onguru Venkaiah and Sanjeevamma at Wanaparthy. They were blessed with ten children: Jeevamma, Arthur, Arnold, Gladys, Ezra, Krupamma, Kanikaramma, and Eliza. However, two girls named Jayasheela died in early childhood. Benjamin died on 11 January 1982, and Sharamma died on 7 July 1991.[7]

Benjamin and Sharamma studied up to seventh class, as no high school was accessible. Nevertheless, that was the highest level of education in 1925. Benjamin studied at AMB Mission School in Wanaparthy, while Sharamma studied at AMB Mission School in Nagarkurnool.

After his schooling, Benjamin got a government job as a postmaster at Wanaparthy. His monthly salary was ₹ 25/- per month, which was a good salary in those days.

After the marriage, they decided to be in full-time ministry as village preachers. As a first step towards achieving their goal in life, they decided to undergo a Bible-training course. Accordingly, in 1930, they went to Shamshabad for a three-year bible course at Bethany MB

---

[7] Interview with P.B. Arnold, President (GC) and son of Pastor Benjamin and Sharamma Perumalla, Shamshabad, 29 October 2020.

Bible Seminary. In 1932, after completing their three-year seminary education, they were appointed as village preachers at Chennaram village and its hamlet, Gollapally hamlet. They worked not only in Gollapally but also in several villages in Wanaparthy taluk. Benjamin *panthulu* used to travel beyond 20 km.

Benjamin and Sharamma had an English education and could read, write, and speak English. Benjamin *panthulu* became very popular among the people in around 30-40 villages around Gollapally. Villagers began to respect him and his word. Accordingly, he began to settle the land, property, and other disputes in his area, which were acceptable to all. He also peacefully solved marital disputes. Generally, they had to offer him gifts when a dispute was settled. Nevertheless, he never accepted any gift. His services were free of cost for all.

Benjamin and Sharamma preached the Word of God to all, irrespective of caste and creed. On their gospel tours, they walked barefoot. In those days, there were no roads and no means of transportation. Sometimes, they took a rest under the shadow of palm trees. Moreover, sometimes, whenever they feel hungry, they eat palm fruits.

Benjamin *panthulu* was always concerned for the poor, needy, oppressed, downtrodden, and lower caste people. Hence, he became known as a person with compassion for all. Moreover, *panthulu* rebuked the oppressions and exploitations against lower caste people. *Panthulu* played a significant role in getting the bondage labourers' freedom in Gollapally village and several villages around it.

There were no schools in any of the villages around and no modern medical facilities for sick people in those days. For any sickness, villagers had to travel to the MB missionary hospital Wanaparthy. Gollapally *panthulu* encouraged villagers to send their children for schooling. Accordingly, he sent children whose parents were willing to send them to missionary schooling for education. Gollapally had no school, blackboard, slate, or pencil. *Panthulu* and *panthulamma* also taught villagers about cleanliness and hygiene. They also encouraged villagers to go to AMB Mission Hospital, Wanaparthy, for their illness.[8]

Panthulamma started educating the children of Gollapally. Without teaching aids, she taught children how to read and write. Over the smooth surface of the sand, she writes alphabets in English and Telugu and numbers with her index finger. The children trace the alphabet and numbers with their index fingers. In this way, she started educating children.

When the slate and slate pencil became available, they purchased several slates and pencils for all the children. They started to teach them to write on slates with slate pencils. Only boys used to come, but only a few girls came. Those who wanted to continue their education were admitted to the AMB Mission School at Wanaparthy. Most children from all castes stopped after receiving education from *panthulamma*.

Benjamin and Sharamma encouraged villagers to drink clean water and clean their surroundings regularly. Cholera and other plagues were common in those days. Benjamin brought awareness among villagers. He also educated them not to eat the flesh of any dead animal.

Benjamin *panthulu* and Sharamma *panthulamma* played a significant role in the origin and growth of the

---

[8] P.B. Arnold, "Gollapally Panthulu and Panthulamma" [Gollapally's pastor and his wife], typed script, Shamshabad, January 2021.

Mennonite Brethren Church in India and the upliftment of the oppressed and marginalised people.

2.7.
The Life and Legacy of
G.Y. Bhaskar (1958 - 2014)

Bhaskar G.Y. – a social worker, politician, and youth leader, was born on 7 July 1958 to Yesurathnam (Ushaiah) and Ramulamma in Shamshabad. He studied at *Zilla Parishath* High School (ZPHS), Shamshabad. Bhaskar earned a Bachelor of Arts degree from Osmania University, Hyderabad. On 19 May 1983, Bhaskar married Dorothy, daughter of K. John and Hannamma. Bhaskar died on 20 June 2014.[9]

Bhaskar was a youth leader in the MB Field Youth Association Shamshabad (MBFAS). As a Chairman of the MBFAS, he initiated the 'Christmas Gifts for Preachers Project' as a token of gratitude for their sacrificial ministry. The project has been active till today. Under his leadership, several 'One-day Youth Retreats' were conducted in the villages of Shamshabad Field to cater to the spiritual needs of the youth. He encouraged the talents of young men and women. Bhaskar also served as the advisor of the MBFAS for several years. Bhaskar's mission in youth ministry was to encourage young men and women to enthusiastically pursue the right relationship with God. In fact, as a youth leader, Bhaskar was responsible for building a sense of community within the church youth and provided an opportunity for spiritual and social development.

Moreover, he was a powerful volleyball player. As a

---

[9] Interview with G. Dorothy Bhaskar, wife of G.Y. Bhaskar, Shamshabad, 2 September 2021.

sports person, Bhaskar encouraged youth to conduct and participate in inter-church volleyball and Cricket tournaments.

In the Bethany MB Church Shamshabad, Bhaskar served as secretary, assistant-secretary, and Sunday school superintendent in several capacities. He served as the Chairman of Bethany MB Church from 2013 to 2014. Bhaskar acquired three acres of land from the GC and MB Property Association to construct a new church building. Accordingly, on 11 May 2014, under the chairmanship of Bhaskar, 'the Ground-breaking Ceremony for Megha Church' was held. Rev. Dr. P.B. Arnold, the President - GC, laid the foundation stone. He was also a delegate to the MB Property Association for several years.

As a politician, Bhaskar played an active role in the Congress Party. In 2001, he was elected a Ward Member of the Grama Panchayati Shamshabad. He completed his Five-year tenure successfully. From 2007 to 2010, he served as the Director of the Narsingi Market Committee.

Bhaskar contributed significantly to the development of the Shamshabad Mission Compound. For instance, he took the initiative to provide Drinking Water (Borewell and water tap connection), street lights, and a road facility. He assisted the impoverished and needy in accessing the social benefit schemes provided by the government. For instance, Bhaskar helped the supporting staff of the MB Centenary Bible College, Shamshabad, to avail of the 'Rajiv Gruha Kalpa Housing Scheme.' He also guided Christians to get jobs in the public sector.

2.8.

The Life and Legacy of
A.S. Caleb (1931 – 2001)

C aleb A.S. – Paramedical Practitioner and Churchman, born on 15 July 1931,[10] at Papireddy Gudem village, near Shadnagar, Ranga Reddy district. His parents, Abbi Sayanna and Kistamma, were farmers. Caleb was the eldest son in the family. He had two sisters and a brother: Chennamma, Rachel, and David.

Caleb married B.P. Padma on May 3, 1960. Padma was the only daughter of Papaiah and Mariamma Bootham. Rev. V.L. Benjamin solemnised their marriage. They were blessed with a son, Daniel (wife – Anitha), and three daughters – Mercy (husband – Jaypaul), Esther Rani (husband – Paul), and Blessy Beulah (husband – Sunil Kumar). Caleb died on 29 July 2001.

From 1939 to 1948, Caleb had schooling from the first to the tenth standard at MB High School Shamshabad. He studied HSC at Priston Institute Jangaon from 1948 to 1949. He had his Bachelor of Science and Master of Arts degrees from Osmania University, Hyderabad. In addition, Caleb completed DMLT Training at Arogyavaram, Chittoor district, Andhra Pradesh, from 1953 to 1954.

---

[10] Interview with A.C. Daniel, son of A.S. Caleb and Journalist, Shamshabad, January 20, 2021; A.S. David, "Ki.she A.S. Caleb gaari kluptha jeevitha charithra" [Brief Biography of Late A.S. Caleb], Manuscript, Shamshabad, 2001.

After his DMLT training, Caleb worked at Osmania Government Hospital, Hyderabad, and Gandhi Government Hospital, Secunderabad. Caleb worked for many years at the Institute of Preventive Medicine (IPM), Narayanaguda, Hyderabad. The Government recognised his skills and commitment and sent him to NIMS to establish a Bio-Chemistry Lab there. After that, Caleb was again transferred to the IPM, where he worked until he retired on 13 July 1989. He was promoted to Gazetted Rank officer at IPM.

Rev. J.H. Lorenz baptised Caleb at Bethany MB Church Shamshabad. He became an active communicant member of the same Church. He served in different capacities in the Bethany MB Church, Shamshabad, and MB Field Association Shamshabad.

In addition, Caleb was very active in the Indian MB Conference. His role and contribution to the emergence and growth of the MB Church are highly appreciated. He served as treasurer of the GC and secretary of the MB Board of Education.

Caleb and his wife, Padma, contributed significantly to the development of MB Mission School Shamshabad. On weekends and vacations, Caleb visited villages to organise health camps to bring awareness of health care, sanitisation, and the pandemic. He distributed medicines to the sick. He had regular medical tours in Papireddy Gudem village. Even today, villagers appreciate his love, generosity, and contribution to the medical field.

His grandson, Dr. Nectar Manohar Abbi, a medical practitioner, continues Caleb's legacy through medical service.

2.9.

The Life and Legacy of
K. Chellaiah Reuben (1932-2021)

C hellaiah Reuben Katikapalle – teacher, preacher, and educationist, was born on 26 April 1932[11] in Madanapally, Chittoor district, Andhra Pradesh. His parents – Katikapalle Philip Reuben and Gnana Sundaramma, worked as teacher-cum-preacher in the London Missionary Society. Reuben married Lakshmi Kantha Jalm, daughter of Mrs. and Dr. A. John. They were blessed with three sons and three daughters – Philip, Patrick Prabhu Charan, Pamela, Paulina, and Prasuna. His wife died in 2002. Chellaiah Reuben was called to glory on 01 December 2021 in Mahabubnagar, Telangana State, India.

Reuben had his schooling at Madanapally and intermediate at Voorhees College, Vellore, in 1952. In 1954, he graduated from Madras Christian College, Tambaram, Chennai. Reuben had a Bachelor of Education from Andhra Christian College, Guntur, Andhra Pradesh. He completed a two-year post-graduation in Christian Education at MB Biblical Seminary, Fresno, USA, in 1970.

The then missionary, John A. Wiebe, encouraged Reuben to render services in the American MB Mission in the south Telangana region. Accordingly, on 12 March 1956, Reuben joined MB Central High

---

11 K. Chellaiah Reuben, "Life History of K. Chellaiah Reuben," in *Mennonite Brethren Theological Graduates with their Life History and Literary Contributions* (1920-2011), compiled by D.N. Purushotham (Hyderabad: G.J. Douglas, 2012), 68.

School, Mahabubnagar, as a teacher. He also worked at MB High School Gadwal and MB High School Devarakonda. In 1990, Reuben retired as a headmaster and correspondent of MBC High School, Mahabubnagar.

As a teacher, he influenced young minds. Students were/are considered the future of the nation and humankind. He played a significant role in the student's life. Reuben brought out the best in students and inspired them to strive for greatness.

Reuben was a gifted writer. He wrote several books, including Jeevitha Chivari Gadiyalu (Telugu), Ten Sermons, etc. Reuben presented a paper on "The Contribution of Christian Educational Institutions in Meeting the Educational Needs of the People of India" at the Mennonite World Conference, Calcutta, 1997.

He was also a prolific preacher. His sermons were received well by the villagers. Reuben worked with Viola Wiebe, mother of Dr. Paul Wiebe, in Christian Education (CE), Sunday School, and other ministry activities.

Reuben served as secretary of the Governing Council of the Conference of the MB Church of India (GC) and MB Board of Education (GC) (for one year), chairman, secretary, and treasurer of MB Field Association Mahabubnagar, vice-chairman, secretary, member of the Calvary MB Church Mahabubnagar for several years. He visited several countries, including the USA, the UK, France, Israel, Japan, the Philippines, and Rome.

2.10.
The Life and Legacy of Daniel E.B.

D aniel E.B. – an evangelist and preacher, was born in 1914 in Ippakunta village, Balmoor Mandal, Nagarkurnool district, to Balaiah and Sitamma Elakonda. His siblings are Elisha, Rathnamma, Manikyamma, Vajramma, Krupaiah, and Johnsundar. In 1934, he married Deevenamma of Mitta Sadagodu village. They were blessed with ten children, five daughters and five sons – Vinolyamma, Jayaprasad, Shakunthalamma, James, Vilashitha, Israel, Elizabeth, Alwis, Varaprada, and Vishwaprasad. [12]

Daniel studied up to the seventh standard. During Daniel F. Berghthold's period, he also studied a one-year theological course at MB Bible School, Nagarkurnool. Later, he was appointed pastor in his native village, Ippakunta, a hamlet of Gattuthumman Panchayath. He also evangelised the villages of Jinkunta, Lazmapur, Mamillapally, Chennaram, and Uppununthala.

Daniel was a simple man who trusted in God. His burning desire was to take the gospel of Jesus Christ to as many people as possible in his time. Daniel applied self-support and self-propagation in gospel outreach and planting churches when he realised the need for native workers in the mission field. He had to spend much, possibly most, of his time working to support himself.

Daniel was best known for his skills in making ox-

---

12 "Saho. E.B. Daniel – Suvartha sevakudu – Ippakunta Gramamu" (Bro. E.B. Daniel, evangelist, Ippakunta village), in *MB Mission Centenary Celebrations Nagarkurnool (1904-2004). Souvenir* (Nagarkurnool: MB Church Nagarkurnool, 2004).

cars. He earned money by making ox-cars, carpentry, and blacksmith work to support himself in witnessing Christ. He was also a farmer. Indeed, the self-supporting ministry was/is a privilege and a joy. It was a privilege for Daniel to dedicate his time and energy to God's ministry. It was/is a joy to serve God's people in all the ways that a self-supporting ministry can. His method of self-supporting ministry is a good role model for evangelists and preachers of this generation.

In 1935, he constructed a *Yedu Sandulamidde* (a typical Telangana rural house made with wooden pillars) where village Christians worship regularly. In 1979, a new church building was constructed in the same place. B.E. Krupaiah, G.P. Paul, Y. Devadanam, and Dr. Theevisamma sponsored the church roof.

Throughout their ministry, Daniel and Deevenamma deeply desired the lost with the gospel of Jesus Christ. They never feel tired of helping village Christians to grow in their faith. They influenced others in positive ways according to biblical standards. Besides evangelism, Daniel promoted village education. He encouraged villagers to send their children to the village school conducted in his house or church.

He is remembered today as an influential, self-supporting evangelist, preacher, and teacher of his time. Daniel and Deevenamma led hundreds of people to faith in Jesus Christ through evangelism and preaching.

2.11.
The Life and Legacy of
Rev. Y.R. Devadanam (1945-2012)

Devadanam Yennamalla "Y.R. Devadanam" – an evangelist, preacher, church planter, Churchman, and social worker. Devadanam was born on 13 March 1945 in Sirsanagandla village Charakonda Mandal, Nagarkurnool district, Telangana State. Devadanam's parents, Pedda Rama Chandraiah (Rajarathnam) and Mutthamma Yennamalla, were the first believers in the village. Devadanam was the first child in a family of two sons and four daughters.

On Friday, 18 June 1971, Devadanam married Kamalamma, the second daughter of Kamtam Jacob (Yakobu) and Rahelamma (Peddamma) of Urukonda village, Kalwaurthy, at MB Church, Urukonda. Rev. P. Paul solemnised their marriage, and Rev. R.R.K. Murthy delivered the wedding sermon.

Devadanam and Kamalamma were blessed with Dayaker, Jayaker, and Prabhaker. On 18 March 2012, Devadanam died in the Government Osmania General Hospital, Hyderabad, due to severe illness.

Devadanam studied at Mennonite Mission High School, Devarakonda, and Government Zilla Parishath School, Devarakonda, Nalgonda district, Telangana. Devadanam earned a three-year Senior Diploma in Theology course from Mennonite Brethren Bible Institute, Shamshabad, from 1969 to 1970 and 1971 to 1973, a Bachelor of Theology degree from the Senate of Serampore College (University) (at Andhra Christian Theological College) from 1989 to 1992.

Deeply touched at age fifteen by Matthew 11:28, Devadanam sought the Lord and confessed all of his sins before Jesus Christ. Shortly after that, he was baptised and joined the Church. Realising the Lord had a work for him in His Glorious ministry, Devadanam enrolled in the three-year studies course mentioned above in Shamshabad in preparation.

Devadanam worked in the MB Conference of India in several capacities and various departments. Soon after completing his three-year Senior Course in Bible studies in Shamshabad, he worked three years as a full-time pastor at Chinna Thundla village, Shamshabad Field, from 1973 to 1975. Next, until 1979, he worked alongside Rev. R. R. K. Murthy and Rev. V. K. Rufus in the Mennonite Brethren Christian Education Ministry (GC).

He is best known for his evangelism and church planting. In the early 1980s, Devadanam faced severe persecution by Hindu Fanatics in the Old City of Hyderabad, who beat him severely and even abducted him to kill. Miraculously, he escaped death. When the local police officers arrested them, Devadanam asked the police officers to release them, and he did not lodge a case against them. He forgave them. Since then, he received respect and honour from people of other faiths.

In 1980, Devadanam, in the name of the Almighty, founded the Faith Mennonite Brethren Church in Chandrayan Gutta, in the Old City of Hyderabad, where he then served as pastor for the remainder of his life. During the 1980s, Devadanam also founded another Mennonite Brethren Church in the Old City of Hyderabad, this time in Arundothi Nagar, Uppuguda, which was in 1994 merged with Baptist Church Hyderabad. Also, during the 1980s, Devadanam served as pastor from time to time at the Central Reserved Police Force Chapel (CRPF) Chandrayan Gutta, Hyderabad. He was also instrumental in constructing the Mennonite Brethren Church in his home village, Sirasanagandla, in 2004.[13] As a Christian Marriage Registrar (Government-issued marriage License), he solemnised over 200 marriages.

Devadanam was commissioned in 1987, ordained on 18 January 1998, at Faith Mennonite Brethren Church, Chandrayan Gutta, as a minister of the Word of God by the Mennonite Brethren Conference of India (GC). He witnessed and led prayers (multi-religious prayers) regularly at various gatherings in the Old City of Hyderabad, more significantly at the historical Charminar, during his years as a pastor in Chandrayan Gutta. Devadanam was a key person in the formation of the 'Old City Christian Welfare Association (Hyderabad)' and the 'United Christian Churches Cemetery Association, South Zone, Hyderabad.'

Devadanam, at different times, served as chairman (1989-1992), Assistant Chairman (2004-2006), secretary (1996-1998), Assistant Secretary (1983-1984 and 1994-1996), member (1998-2000), and Evangelism-chairman (2002-2004) of the Mennonite Brethren Field Association Shamshabad.

He also attended several international Mennonite gatherings, such as the Mennonite World Conference in Nepal in 1988 and Kolkata in 1997.

He also served the young people of the Mennonite Brethren Field Youth Association Shamshabad in various capacities. Devadanam was a member of the Mennonite Brethren Peace Committee for eight years.

---

[13] Interview with Y.D. Kamalamma, wife of Rev. Y.R. Devadanam, Chandrayan Gutta, Hyderabad, 18 February 2021.

He was also a delegate to the Governing Council of the Conference of the MB of India. Devadanam served as a vice-president of the Old City Christian Welfare Association from 1998 to 2012.

Besides evangelism and church planting, Devadanam also engaged in the larger society in other ways. For instance, he was at different times a member of the Andhra Pradesh Voluntary Health Association (1995), a general secretary of the New Indira Nagar Residents Welfare Association, a Maithri Volunteer of the South Zone Police Station of the Old City of Hyderabad, and a member of Peace Committee of South Zone Police Station of the Old City Hyderabad (1996-2012). Devadanam also served as a Convener of the Hyderabad Congress Minority Committee (a national political party), promoting peace in the Old City of Hyderabad.

Devadanam received respect from people for his ministry as a teacher, and they always identified him as a *panthulu* (male-teacher) more than a Christian Preacher.

2.12.

The Life and Legacy of
Rev. Hannah Joseph (1938-2021)

Hannah Joseph – woman leader, churchwoman, Bible teacher, and social worker, was born in 1938 in Petthulla village, Ibrahimpatnam, Ranga Reddy district, Telangana State, to Pochaiah and Peddamma Kompally.[14] Hannah was the third daughter in the family. She lost her father at a young age. Her family moved to Shamshabad in 1947 with the help of Rev. John Lorenz, the then-resident missionary at Shamshabad. On 21 December 1968, Hannah married S.J. Joseph of Vempadu village, Needamanur Mandal, Nalgonda district. Hannah and Joseph were blessed with two children: Kemuel and Lavanya. Hannah died on 4 June 2021, around 8:30 pm, at her residence, Shamshabad.

Hannah had her Middle School level education at Shamshabad from 1947 to 1951 and High School level education at MB Central Highschool, Mahabubnagar, in 1951. Hannah was the first Telugu woman to enrol in the G.Th. course at Union Biblical Seminary, Yeotmal, Maharashtra. She earned a Master of Arts (Public Administration) from Osmania University in 1981. She also completed a library science course in 1965.

During her schooling at Shamshabad, she was baptised by Rev. V.L. Benjamin at Bethany MB Church Shamshabad in 1951. Since then, she has become a communicant member of the Church. Hannah worked

---

[14] Interview with S.J. Joseph, Director of Christian Concern Mission, Shamshabad, 25 September 2021

as the first female evangelist of the Governing Council of the Conference of the MB Church of India from 1963 to 1968. She served as a librarian and Counsellor at MB High School Hughestown, Hyderabad, from 1965 to 1967. Then, she served as a Bible Teacher at MB Bible Institute, Shamshabad, from 1967 to 1982.

Later, Hannah and her husband, Joseph, established the 'Christian Concern Mission (CCM)' ministry to reach out to needy, poor girl children and young people in 1981. They started a hostel for girls and provided education. Many girls were benefited.

Hannah served among women through the MB Field Women Association Shamshabad. She was one of the first MB Ordained women in India in 2008.

She held different positions in the MB Conference from 1963 to 2016. Hannah was the first national chairperson of the MB Women Conference in India. She served as President of the All-India MB Women Conference.

She actively organised women's programmes during the Mennonite World Conference 1997 in Kolkata, India. Hannah represented the Andhra Pradesh Christian Council, the National Council of Churches in India (NCCI), and the Christian Evangelical Education Foundation of India (CEEFI). She also visited several foreign countries and witnessed Christ.

2.13.
The Life and Legacy of
Rev. Vankeshwaram Isaac (1938-2016)

Isaac Vankeshwaram – evangelist, pastor, orator, author, and Churchman, was born on 15 November 1938, at Thawklapuram village, Devarakonda Taluk, Nalgonda district.[15] Isaac's parents, Veeraiah and Marthamma Vankeshwaram, were pioneer Christian believers in Thawklapuram village.

In 1953, Isaac married Esther Rani. Solomon Raju, Manohar, Vijay Prasad, Shoba Rani, and Swarupa Rani were born to Isaac. Isaac died on 29 February 2016.

Isaac had his schooling at Mennonite Brethren Highschool Devarakonda. He studied SLC. After school, Isaac worked as an electrician at Nagarjunasagar Project, built on Krishna, 42 km from Devarakonda.

Isaac's parents dedicated him to God's ministry. Accordingly, they encouraged him to attend Devarakonda MB Mission Station for theological training. After successful seminary training, Isaac was appointed as the Pastor of Bethaniya MB Church Thawklapuram. He served as a pastor there until he died in 2016.

---

[15] P. Agustin, "Late. Rev. V. Isaac pastor gaari sakshyam" [Testimony of Late. Rev. V. Isaac pastor] (Devarakonda: MB Church Thawklapuram, 2016); Augustine, Pachigolla, "Thawklapuram Bethaniya M.B. church charithra" [History of Bethaniya M.B. church Thawklapuram] (Devarakonda: MB Church Thawklapuram, 2016); Interview with Pachigolla Augustine, Pastor of MB Church Thawklapuram, Kalwakurthy, 12 February 2018.

Isaac was a gifted writer and orator. He used his talents to reach illiterate villagers and brought many to Christ. For instance, He wrote a play on 'Jesus' Birth, Death, and Resurrection' suitable to villagers. Isaac and his team travelled from village to village to perform this play for three nights. On the first day, the play narrates Jesus's birth, the second day explores Jesus's death, and the third day portrays Christ's resurrection. Isaac served as one of the members of the editorial board – *Suvarthamani*. He wrote several articles in *Suvarathami*.

The Governing Council of the Conference of the MB Church of India (GC) ordained Isaac to minister the Word of God. As a chairman, he oversaw the MB Congregations of MB Field Association Devarakonda for many years. From 2006 to 2016, Isaac served several times as vice-chairman of the MB Board of Evangelism and Church Ministries (GC) as a co-opted member of GC and CRC (Committee of Reference and Counsel).

Apart from his pastoral duties, through the village school's non-formal education, he taught many villagers how to read and write irrespective of their caste and creed. He encouraged children to go to MB Mission School Devarakonda for formal education. He also taught tanning to many villagers. In turn, these villagers made money through their work.

2.14.

The Life and Legacy of
Jakkula Lingaiah (1906-1978)

Jakkula Lingaiah "Golla Lingaiah" - shepherd, truth-seeker, and evangelist was born in 1906 in a small village, Chedurpally, of MB Mission Field Kalwakurthy, Telangana State, India. He was born and raised in a Hindu family who belonged to the sheep-grazing *Erra Golla* caste,[16] the primary and topmost in the hierarchy of sub-castes of *Gollas* (*Yadavs*). Based on their complexion, they are classified as *Erra Gollas*.

His parents, Ramaiah and Ramulamma Jakkula were illiterates and practised their traditions by keeping thousands of goats and sheep flocks. Their main occupation was farming and sheep rearing. Lingaiah married Mallamma and was blessed with five daughters and three sons.

In the 1960s, Lingaiah's elder son and daughter-in-law, Mrs. and Mr. J.L. John, rendered their services at the MB Medical Centre, Jadcherla, as a Lab Technician and Staff Nurse, respectively. His second son, Rev. J.L. David, is the Executive Director of the Mennonite Brethren Development Organization (MBDO).

In those days, *Gollas* were illiterate and had no practice of wearing shirts; instead, they kept Gongadi (blanket), which was weaved from sheep wool, on their shoulders. Moreover, most of the Gollas in Telangana State lead a settled life. However, some of them still lead

---

[16] A community designated by the Government of India as the Other Backward Class (OBC).

a nomadic life. Wherever they are settled – forests, villages, and urban areas – they lead a much better social status and dignity than other castes. They are identified in society as animal rearers and grazers.[17]

Lingaiah was the eldest son in the family. He had the responsibility of looking after their sheep. Hence, Lingaiah was often away from home while grazing sheep. Jakkula David says, "In 1932, one night, as he looked after the sheep flocks, he saw a cross-type lightning in the sky. He had never witnessed this kind of lightning before. Usually, lightning would be like a jig jag. Lingaiah was wondering what this is cross-type. He asked the Hindu religious priests, but they could not explain."[18] He did not give up his quest to seek the truth about this beautiful creation's Creator. As years passed, he got no answer from either Hindu Priests or great people.

However, one afternoon, while working in their agricultural field, he encountered a stranger who transformed his life. On his way to another village, the stranger stopped to have lunch, considering water to drink. Lingaiah was known for his hospitality. He asked the stranger what his name was and what his profession was. The stranger replied that his name was P.V. Abraham *panthulu,* a Christian evangelist who preached the Good News of Jesus Christ, travelling from village

---

[17] It is because of their animal rearing occupation that they could establish good socio-economic relations with the upper and lower castes of the society. They directly sell their animals, dairy products, blankets, and animal litter for manure to all classes of society. No class or caste in the society observes social differences with them while purchasing the dairy products from the *Gollas.*

[18] J.L. David, "Jakkula Lingaiah (Golla Lingaiah 1906-1978). A Shepherd Boy Heard a Call of Heavenly Shepherd" *MB Mission Centenary Celebrations Nagarkurnool (1904-2004). Souvenir* (Nagarkurnool: MB Church Nagarkurnool, 2004).

to village. By inspiring his reply, Lingaiah asked Abraham *panthulu* about the Creator of this beautiful creation. He also narrated about lightning, which he had seen in the past. Abraham *panthulu* was a committed and faithful servant of Lord Jesus Christ. *Panthulu* explained God, the Creator and the creation, the incarnation of Jesus Christ, His earthly ministry, His cross of Calvary, His crucifixion, His death, and His resurrection. Instantly, Lingaiah felt peaceful as his longing doubts have been clarified.

Moreover, Lingaiah realised he was a sinner and needed redemption that was possible only through the blood of Jesus Christ. Hence, Lingaiah repented, confessed, and believed in Jesus without any delay. Furthermore, he accepted Jesus Christ as his Saviour and Lord by witnessing the baptism.

Through his ministry, Abraham *panthulu* significantly impacted the lives of people of his time. For instance, Lingaiah's conversion into the MB Church portrays the role and contribution of local workers in transforming people's lives, irrespective of caste and creed. Abraham was nicknamed '*Yeddu Abraham Panthulu*' (Ox Abraham *Panthulu*) because his means of transportation was an ox.

The then missionaries, D.F. Bergthold, Wiebe, P.V. Balzar, and H. Warkentin, were inspired by hearing about Lingaiah's conversion experience to the Christian faith. They encouraged him to witness Jesus Christ among his relatives and others from the *Gollas* community. Accordingly, missionaries – H. Warkentin and P.V. Balzar took Lingaiah to several villages to share his testimony and personal experience with the Lord and Saviour Jesus Christ. His life and testimony influenced many people to become Christians. Accordingly, Lingaiah became a co-partner with the MB missionaries in the growth of the MB Church in India.

However, after his conversion, his people and in-laws persecuted Lingaiah. They accused that he converted into a religion of low caste people. He witnessed social discrimination – he was not allowed to take drinking water from his well, which he dug by himself. Moreover, they wanted to separate his wife Mallamma, but she stood firmly with him. After fifteen years, his wife also embraced the Christian faith.[19]

In 1959, they constructed a church building in Chedurpally and supported the pastor. Despite persecutions and temptations, they witnessed Jesus Christ powerfully until they were called into heavenly glory. Jakkula Lingaiah died in April 1978, and Mallamma died in November 2000.

---

[19] Interview with J.L. David, second son of Jakkula Lingaiah, Jadcherla, 28 December 2020

2.15.

The Life and Legacy of
Rev. N.P. James and Deevenamma

James Naikal "N.P. James" – pastor and Bible teacher, was born on 25 May 1927 in Yenugabala village, Yemmiganur, Kurnool district, Andhra Pradesh, to Prasangi and Meramma. James married Deevenamma on 31 July 1953. God blessed James and Deevenamma with six children: three sons and three daughters. He was baptised on 04 April 1949. On 28 October 1967, James was ordained as a minister of the Word of God at Bethany MB Church, Shamshabad. James received the heavenly call on 14 July 2012.[20]

James studied at the Primary School, Yenugabala (1934-40) and MB Mission Schools in Gadwal, Wanaparthy, and Mahabubnagar. James and Deevenamma completed a Graduate in Theology (G.Th.) course from the Baptist Seminary Ramayapatnam (1954-57). James completed a Bachelor of Divinity degree from Union Biblical Seminary, Yeothmal (1962-66), and a Master of Arts (Theology) from MB Seminary, Fresno, California, USA.

James wrote his Master's thesis on "The Contribution of the Mennonite Brethren Bible Institute Shamshabad to the Mennonite Brethren Conference in India, 1920-

---

[20] Yennamalla Jayaker, "Rev. N.P. James: The First National Principal of MB Bible School Shamshabad," (paper presented at MB Centenary Bible College, Shamshabad, 30 January 2018).

1970,"[21] MB Biblical Seminary, 1973.

James served in many different positions at the MB Conference over the years. From 1950 to 1953, he worked as a schoolteacher at the MB School Wanaparthy. James was the First National Principal of the MB Bible Institute, Shamshabad (now MBCBC) from 1970 to 1971 and from 1974 to 1980.

James, at different times, served as Chairman (1975-77), Treasurer (1968-70 and 1970-71) of the Governing Council of the Conference of the Mennonite Brethren Church of India (GC), and Property Director of the MB Property Association Pvt. Ltd., (1957-82). He worked as the pastor of the Bethany MB Church Shamshabad (1982-86) and Bethlehem MB Church Malakpet (1987-2012).

Deevenamma was an evangelist, preacher, and woman leader. On 28 July 1932, Deevenamma was born to Joshua and Chandrakala Munagalshetty in Addakula village, Mahabubnagar district, Telangana State. She attended MB Mission School (primary and middle school), Wanaparthy, and MB Central School (High school), Mahabubnagar. Deevenamma promoted women's ministry at the grassroots level at the MB Conference. Moreover, she played a key role in the women's ministry at the local, field, and conference levels. Deevenamma was known for her hospitality, compassion ministry, and personal evangelism. Deevenamma and James, throughout their ministry, helped the poor and subaltern people.

---

[21] N.P. James, "The Contribution of the Mennonite Brethren Bible Institute Shamshabad to the Mennonite Brethren Conference in India, 1920-1970" (M.A. thesis, M.B. Biblical Seminary, 1973).

2.16.

The Life and Legacy of
Rev. M.B. John (1909-2002)

John Medari "John M.B." – preacher and churchman, was born on 21 September 1908, at Gudipally village, Devarakonda, Nalgonda district, to Buchaiah and Muthyalamma Medari. John lost his mother when he was seven years old. His father sent him to his uncle, Moses, a pastor at Mandapoor village. Accordingly, John became a faithful and dutiful shepherd boy in three years of his stay with his uncle from 1915 to 1917.

John married K. Krupamma, daughter of Mr. and Mrs. K. Benjamin of Nalgonda, on 23 March 1933. They were blessed with four sons and five daughters. Krupamma died on 14 January 1999, and John died on 29 July 2002 in Hyderabad.

His uncle, Moses, admitted John to the Mennonite Brethren Mission School Nagarkurnool in early 1918. At that time, there was no mission school at Devarakonda. However, at the end of 1918, the MB Mission school was opened in Devarakonda. Hence, John returned to Devarakonda and completed the III form there in 1926. He completed his high school studies at the Coles Memorial High School, Kurnool, in 1932. [22]

John had a three-year Bible School training at Nagarkurnool from 1926 to 1929, a one-year Bible Training at the Allahabad Oriental Missionary Society from 1949 to 50, and one semester of Bible training at

---

[22] Arthur Dalavai, *The Tallest Tree in the IMB Field: The History of Dr. Rev. M.B. John* (n.p.: Son and Daughters of Dr. Rev. M.B. John, 2003).

Fresno Seminary Fresno, California, USA, from September 1960 to February 1961. Besides, the Hindustan Bible Institute of Madras, India, conferred the Doctor of Divinity degree on 10 October 1997.

He worked as a teacher at MB Mission School Devarakonda from 1932 to 1936. He left school and joined the PWD office in Pendlipakala as a clerk from 1936 to 1944.

On 8 August 1944, John was appointed headmaster of the American MB Mission School at Mahabubnagar and continued in the same position until 1948. John was appointed as pastor of the Calvary MB Church Mahabubnagar in 1949. On 8 July 1953, John was ordained at Calvary MB Church Mahabubnagar.

Rev. John became the first national chairman of the Governing Council of the Conference of Mennonite Brethren Church of India (GC) from 1960 to 1961. He was elected GC Chairman for five terms: 1960-61, 1962-63, 1963-64, 1973-74, and 1974-75.

John attended several international gatherings. He was a Fraternal Delegate from MB Churches in India to the MB Centennial Conference (1860-1960) at Reedly, California, USA from 13-16 November 1960. John also visited several MB Churches in the United States and Canada for fellowship, preaching, and presenting MB Churches' activities in India. Again, he visited the USA to attend the Mennonite Presidium Meeting of the World Mennonite Conference held from July 2-9, 1975.

2.17.

The Life and Legacy of
Pastor P. Joshua and Sharamma

Joshua and Sharamma P.[23] were the village preachers, evangelists, and teachers at Agapally village, Ibrahimpatnam, Ranga Reddy district, Telangana State, India. On 14 January 1892, Joshua was born in Kanapur village, near Ibrahimpatnam, while Sharamma was born in Agapally in the Dasari family on 4 June 1904.

From 1908 to 1915, Joshua studied up to the fourth standard at MB mission boarding school Malakpet, India's first American MB Mission Station. He had his schooling under the guidance of Principal Miss Catharine Lorenz. At the same time, Sharamma studied at MB Boarding School, Shamshabad. Moreover, after school education, Joshua had a theological course at Bible Seminary, Ramayapatnam, from 1915 to 1918.

In 1919, Rev. Gandham Samuel Douglas solemnised their marriage at MB Church, Shamshabad. Later, they worked as preachers at Lemoor village and then transferred to Agapally village. Due to severe persecution by Muslims, no Christian preacher stayed for a long time in Agapally village because there was Muslim domination (from 1310 to 1948) in the erstwhile Hyderabad. Joshua was a bold preacher, for he withstood persecution and preached the love of Jesus Christ to poor Dalits. A church building was constructed at Agapally in 1942.

---

[23] "A Brief Life History of Late P. Joshua and Sharamma," *MB Mission Centenary Celebrations Nagarkurnool (1904-2004). Souvenir* (Nagarkurnool: MB Church Nagarkurnool, 2004).

Sharamma was a multi-talented woman. She was a singer, songwriter, and storyteller. Also, Sharamma was an expert in *Burrakatha,*[24] a Telugu folk art form of oral storytelling. She narrated Bible stories like *Nayaman* (Namaan), Queen Esther, and *Poola Gampa* in *Burrakatha* form. Sharamma had a good memory because she memorised more than 30 chapters from the Bible at once. She received a prize for reciting Psalm 119 at the MB Convention.

On the other hand, Joshua evangelised in Agapally village and about 12 surrounding villages. His means of transportation was a bicycle. He was popularly known as *"Kirashthan Panthulu."* Because, besides evangelism, he taught poor children how to read and write. Most of the boys worked as bonded labourers without education in those days. Hence, through village schools, he imparted non-formal education to children. Then, they encouraged villagers to send their children to MB Mission Boarding School, Shamshabad, for formal education. Accordingly, from Agapally and surrounding

---

[24] *Burra Katha* or *Burrakatha* is a Telugu folk art form of oral storytelling. *Burra* refers to tambura, a musical string instrument with a hollow shell, and *Katha* means a story. Thus, *Burra Katha* is an art of storytelling in which the narrator plays tambura while narrating. *Burra Katha,* a narrative art, consists of prayers, dance, songs, poems, and jokes). The narrative topic would be a mythological issue or a social one. *Burra Katha* is prominent mainly in the rural areas of Andhra Pradesh, Telangana, and Karnataka states. In Telangana, *Burra Katha* is also known as *Tamboora Katha* or *Saradakatha.* It is believed that the art played such an influential role in conveying a sense of awakening among the people that the British banned its performances in Madras Presidency, and the ruler of the Hyderabad State, the Nizam, too banned it in his domain. Tejaswi Marthi, "Keeping Burra Katha Alive in the Wave of Impersonal Storytelling Art Forms" *The Hindu* (Vijayawada) August 19, 2019.

villages, over 100 children studied at MB Mission School, Shamshabad. Later, they became able leaders and committed pastors.

Joshua heard the voices of Dalits and significantly contributed to their upliftment. He liberated many children from the clutches of bonded slavery. In turn, Village Officers, *Muslim Patwari, Police Patel*,[25] and other high-caste people persecuted him. However, he did not give up his work. As a result, many who studied at Mission Boarding School Shamshabad became teachers, nurses, and bus conductors, and some held high-rank positions in government offices.

In addition, from Agapally village, many became God's servants, like Joseph and Leyamma Koppy (in Agapally), Rev. Mathaiah, and Rathnamma Nousu (in Peddathundla village), Mark and Shanthamma Borra (in Manchala village), John and Rebecca Borra (Gourelli village), Rev. D.P. John (in Agapally), and Mrs. C. Shanthamma Charles (Nayapool), from Kanapur village P. Andraiah, and P. Simon and Manikyamma.

Pastor Joshua and Sharamma helped the poor and needy throughout their ministry. They are role models to contemporary mission practitioners. They significantly extended the MB church and brought social change through their holistic mission approach.

---

[25] The *patwari* was to look after the village revenue administration, revenue collection, and the maintenance of revenue records. The police *Patel*, who was in charge of the general administration, looked after law and order, registered the births and deaths, and reported crimes to the higher police officers.

2.18.

The Life and Legacy of
Rev. Y.D. Kamalamma (1948-2021)

Kamalamma Devadanam Yennamalla "Y.D. Kamalamma" - a senior woman preacher, leader, and evangelist, was born on 20 March 1948[26] to Yakobu and Rahelamma Kamtam in Urukonda, Kalwakurthy, Nagarkurnool district. On Friday, 18 June 1971, Kamalamma married Rev. Y.R. Devadanam, the eldest son of Pedda Ramchandriah (Rajarathnam) and Muthamma Yennamalla, Sirasanagandla village, Charakonda Mandal, Nagarkurnool district, Telangana State, at MB Church Urukonda. Rev. P. Paul solemnised their marriage. Rev. R.R.K. Murthy delivered a marriage sermon.

On Monday, 5 April 2021, she passed away at five o'clock in the evening due to a massive brain stroke after a gradual decline in health. Her husband, Rev. Y.R. Devadanam (2012), grandson Y. Karunaker Prabhaker (2014), and younger son, Prabhaker (2017), predeceased her.

Kamalamma was survived by two sons – Y.D. Dayaker and Rev. Dr. Y.D. Jayaker; three daughters-in-law – Barathamma Dayaker, Samadhanam Jayaker, and Umarani Prabhaker; seven grandchildren – Y.D. Rathnam (wife – Y. Elizabeth Rathnam), Y.D. Devaprakash, Y.D. Krupaker, Y.J. Kamalaker, Y.J. Joyson, Y.P. Dinaker and Y.P. Quity. She was also

---

[26] Interview with Y.D. Dayaker, vice-chairman of Faith MB Church, Chandrayan Gutta, Hyderabad, 10 April 2021.

survived by three sisters and a brother: M. Kistamma Laxmaiah, G. Kalawathi Daniel, K. Vimalamma Shyamsunder, and K. Abraham.

Kamalamma studied at MB Mission School (1-8 classes) and Zilla Parishath Girls' High School (ninth class) in Devarakonda, Nalgonda district. Rev. Gandham Albert Samuel, Devarakonda, encouraged her to pursue education. After schooling, she worked in a Government Department in Amrabad, Achampet. However, after her marriage, Kamalamma resigned from her Government job and devoted herself to full-time ministry. She completed a three-year Senior Diploma in Theology course at the Mennonite Brethren Bible Institute, Shamshabad, in 1973.

Kamalamma worked in the Mennonite Brethren Conference of India in several different capacities over the years. In 1973, Devadanam and Kamalamma were appointed full-time ministers at Chinna Thundla village, Shamshabad Field. Kamalamma also worked as a tailoring instructor and art and craft teacher at Mennonite Brethren Bible Institute, Shamshabad, from 1975 to 1980. Then, they left Shamshabad for Chandrayan Gutta, Hyderabad, and lived there until their death.

In the 1980s, Devadanam and Kamalamma, in the name of the Almighty, founded the Faith Mennonite Brethren Church in Chandrayan Gutta and Shalem MB Church Arundothi Nagar, Uppuguda, in the Old City of Hyderabad. They then served as Preachers of the Faith MB Church for the remainder of their life.

On 7 November 2008, Kamalamma was ordained as a minister of the Word of God by the Mennonite Brethren Conference of India (GC). As a woman leader, she witnessed and led prayers regularly at various women's gatherings in the Old City of Hyderabad and Shamshabad Field. Kamalamma, at different times, served as Chairman, Secretary, Assistant Secretary, and Advisor of the Mennonite Brethren Women Field Association, Shamshabad.

Kamalamma was best known for personal evangelism. Besides evangelism, she also engaged in the task of providing non-formal education to children and adults in her respective areas. Kamalamma also significantly contributed to women's empowerment by teaching tailoring skills to women. She established a 'Tailoring Training Centre' for women in her house,[27] Chandrayan Gutta. Memories of Kamalammas' sacrificial work remain in people's hearts.

Devadanam and Kamalamma received respect from all communities for their ministry as teachers. For instance, people of other faiths always identified Devadanam as *panthulu* (male-teacher) and Kamalamma as *panthulamma* (female-teacher) more than Christian Preachers.

---

[27] Yennamalla Jayaker, "Obituary: Life and Legacy of Rev. Y. Kamalamma Devadanam (1948-2021)," Chandrayan Gutta, Hyderabad, April 14, 2021.

2.19.
The Life and Legacy of
P. Karuna Shree Joel (1964-1996)

Karuna Shree Joel – theologian, preacher, writer, and woman leader, was born on 8 February 1964 at the MB Mission Hospital, Mission Compound, Wanaparthy. She was the eldest daughter of S.S. Krupaiah and B. D. Kanthamma Krupaiah. In 1985, Karuna Shree married P. Menno Joel. God blessed them with three children: a son and two daughters. On 7 July 1996, [28] while returning home, Karuna Shree and her eight-month-old daughter, Sneha, died in a two-wheeler accident on the Himayat Sagar reservoir road, Rajendra Nagar, which is 5 km distance from Shamshabad. They were thrown from their two-wheeler (scooter) into the Himayat Sagar reservoir.

Karuna Shree studied from kindergarten to second class at MB Central High School, Mahabubnagar, and from the fourth to tenth class at MB High School, Mission Compound, Wanaparthy. She completed her Intermediated education at the Government Junior College, Wanaparthy.

After her senior intermediate, Karuna Shree had pre-theology studies at MB Bethany Bible School, Shamshabad. She was a brilliant student. Karuna Shree earned a Bachelor of Theology degree (from the South India Biblical Seminary, Anandgiri, Bangarpet, Karnataka) and a Bachelor of Divinity degree (at Andhra

---

[28] Gary Hardway, "India Women's Leader, 31. Dies in Vehicle Accident," *Mennonite Weekly Review* (August 1, 1996): 3.

Christian Theological College, Secunderabad, Telangana State) in 1990. She was the first MB woman to earn a Master of Theology degree (in Christian Ministry) from the Senate of Serampore College (University) in 1994.

Karuna Shree held several different positions in the MB Conference. She served as executive secretary of the MB Women's Conference, as editor of *Suvarthamani*, and as a lecturer in homiletics and pastoral ministries at MBC Bible College, Shamshabad. Karuna Shree was the first female MB ambassador to the Christian Conference of Asia.[29] She and her husband attended the 12th Mennonite World Conference in Winnipeg, Canada. Karuna Shree also visited several other countries, including the USA, the Philippines, Indonesia, and Taiwan.

Karuna Shree promoted and encouraged women's ministry. The empowerment of women is essential to achieve sustainable development. Ensuring sustainable development requires women's empowerment and equal involvement in decision-making. She believed that when women are empowered, they empower society. With concerns for their families, the entire community of women plays a significant role in developing society. Karuna Shree encouraged women to explore their gifts for the betterment of the church and society.

Karuna Shree was an eloquent preacher. She preached at local, regional, national, and international levels with a message of hope and encouragement. Her sermons challenged the role of women and men in Christ's mission. Karuna Shree and Menno Joel served as Assistant Director and Director of the MB Christian

---

[29] D.N. Purushotham, ed., "Life History of Karunasree Joel (1964–96)," in *Mennonite Brethren Theological Graduates with their Life History and Literary Contributions* (Hyderabad: G.J. Douglas, 2012), 303–307.

Education (GC). They conducted several retreats and seminars in MB Churches across India to cater to the needs of children, youth, and women. Also, she was a writer. Karuna Shree composed several Christian hymns and wrote several articles.

Karuna Shree's life of obedience, commitment, and courage is a model for all who claim to be agents of change in church and society. She was a woman leader with desires and dreams, faults and fears, who gave her life unconditionally to serve the master, Jesus Christ. Commemorating the life story of Karuna Shree Joel has been a highly formative influence in the lives of Christian women for centuries.

2.20.
The Life and Legacy of
Rev. M. J. Krupaiah (1944-2020)

Krupaiah Masku "M.J. Krupaiah" – an educator, teacher, lay-pastor, and administrator was born on 7 July 1944 at Kappapahad village,[30] Ibrahimpatnam Mandal, Ranga Reddy district, Telangana State Kappapahad was his mother's native village. His parents are Jangaiah and Jangamma Masku of Chinnatoondla village, Yacharam Mandal, Ranga Reddy district. Krupaiah was the family's eldest, with four brothers and a sister.

Kruapaiah married B.A. Rose Margaret on 12 May 1967. She worked as a teacher at MB High School, Shamshabad, from 1 July 1967 to 31 July 2005. Krupaiah and Rose Margaret were blessed with four children and seven grandchildren. Two daughters – Parimala (husband – O. Pavithra Sagar), Nirmala (husband – D.E. Hermon), and two sons – David (wife – B. Sunitha) and Peter Victor (wife – N. Pavani). His grandchildren are O. Samuel Zadok, O. Sarojini Krupa Varshini, D. Akhil Thomas, D. Lisa Margaret, M. Preritha, M. Daniel Shaun, and M. Kemuel Seth. On 22 August 2020, Krupaiah died in his residence, Shamshabad.

Krupaiah spent six years in Hyderabad city with his parents while working there. His father, Jangaiah, taught Krupaiah to read and write. In 1948, there was unrest in Hyderabad city as the Indian Government launched a

---

[30] Nanem Mathews David, "Shraddhanjali" [Tributes], printed pamphlet, Balapur, Ranga Reddy district, 2020.

'Police Action' against the Nizam named 'Operation Polo' to overthrow his rule and liberate the non-Muslims. Hence, Krupaiah's family left Hyderabad for their native village, Chinnatoondla. Hence, he lived in the same village for the next six years. He was attracted to *Veedhi Bhagavatham* (Street Play), a Telangana folk art. Traditionally, *Veedhi Bhagavatham* performances took place on thatched stages in the centre of villages or on the outskirts of villages. *Veedhi* means open spaces or streets. Devotees or *Bhagathas* dance, hence it is known as *Veedhi Bhagavatham*. Soon, he became a famous actor, as he had a good memory of it. Since he could deliver dialogue fluently without script, he used to play the main hero character in the play.

One of his cousins advised Krupaiah that *Veedhi Bhagavatham* might not be helpful to him. He further motivated Krupaiah to go to Shamshabad Mission Compound to study. "My parents were financially not sound enough to send me to Shamshabad for formal education… since I had no money, I decided to run away from the village for Shamshabad…" says Krupaiah, M.J.[31] Accordingly, at the age of 12, sometime in the first week of July 1954, he and his friend, G.B. Jacob, left their village for Shamshabad.

Krupaiah was brilliant in his studies, completing eight years of course within five years, i.e., from 1954 to 1959 at Shamshabad. In March 1956, when he was in eighth class, he was baptised by Rev. V.L. Benjamin, MB Church Shamshabad. In July 1959, Krupaiah was admitted to MBC High School, Mahabubnagar. He completed his HSC in 1962 and PUC at Nanakram Bhagavan Das College in 1963. He had three Bachelor's

---

[31] Interview with M.J. Krupaiah, Advisor of MB Field Association Shamshabad, 14 March 2017.

degrees, four Master's degrees from Osmania University, and a Bachelor of Divinity from the Senate of Serampore College. Also, Krupaiah studied a one-year G.Th. course at MB Bible Institute, Shamshabad (1962-1963).

Krupaiah worked as a clerk at MB Bible Institute, Shamshabad, from 1963 to 1965. He worked as an LDC at Karimnagar in the APSEB department (1964-65). From 1965 until retirement in 2002, he worked as a teacher in MB High School Shamshabad. After his retirement, he worked as a lecturer at St. Thomas College of Education in Gadwal (2003-2005) and Treasurer at MBC Bible College, Shamshabad (2005-2009).[32]

Krupaiah was ordained as the Minister of the Word of God by the MB Conference of India on 30 December 2001 at MB Church Muchinthala, Shamshabad Field. Since 1965, he has been active in the local Church, Field, and Conference levels. In different capacities, he served as a lay-pastor for over 20 years at MB Church Muchinthala village, near Shamshabad.

He also served as chairman and assistant chairman of Bethany MB Church and in other capacities for many years. He also served as chairman and vice-chairman of the MB Field Association Shamshabad for several years. At the Conference level, Krupaiah rendered his services as a member of the Board of Theological Education, MB Property Association, Convention Committee, etc.

---

[32] "A Brief History of Rev. M.J. Krupaiah in his own words as told to Mr. O. Pavithra Sagar," Printed Pamphlet, Shamshabad, August 2020.

2.21.
The Life and Legacy of
Rev. M.C. Laban and Manikyamma

Laban Maddela "M.C. Laban" – preacher, evangelist, and Churchman was born on 19 November 1906 to Chinnaiah and Veeramma Maddela in Telugu Pally village, near Devarakonda, Telangana State, India. He married Bandi Manikyamma. They were blessed with three children – Devadanam, Suvarna, and Prasadam.

After their marriage, he decided to be God's Minister. Laban and Manikyamma were appointed as Preachers in Konda Bheemanapally, a village close to the MB Mission station Devarakonda. They were faithful and dedicated ministers of God.

Laban and Manikyamma had love and compassion for the poor, needy, and marginalised communities. Every month, he received a sum of five rupees as an honorarium for his service. Laban used to buy sweets and gifts for the poor children, particularly boarding schoolgirls and boys, out of this little money.

Laban and Manikyamma visited several villages of the Devarakonda mission area barefoot to reach villagers with the good news of Jesus Christ. Often, they use ox-car. They preach the gospel and educate the poor and marginalised children, youth, and adults, including women and men.

From 1972 to 1990, he served as Pastor of MB Zion Church, Mission Compound, Devarakonda. Though he was a resident Pastor, he gave more importance to gospel tours throughout the week. Every day, he used to visit villages with the gospel. From its inception, MB Zion

Church has emphasised gospel outreach programmes. The Church has two outreach programmes, 'Week of Witness' (A group that spends a week and covers as many villages as with the gospel) and 'Sunday Gospel Tour' (Every Sunday evening). Laban was active in these outreach programmes.

Moreover, he became instrumental in constructing the church buildings in the Devarakonda area. He motivated many young men and women for God's ministry. As a result, many went for Bible training.

Laban rendered his services to the development of the Devarakonda Field and the MB Conference, for he served as a chairman (1979-80) and vice-chairman (1980-83, 1983-85) of the Governing Council of the Conference of the MB Church of India.[33] Laban died on April 4, 2000.

On the other hand, his wife, Manikyamma *panthulamma*, worked among the womenfolk. She taught Bible stories and encouraged women to recite or memorise bible verses. Throughout their life, they were faithful to God.

---

[33] Interview with M.J. Purushotham, pastor MB Church Neelam Nagar, Mallepally, Devarakonda, 14 September 2021.

2.22.

The Life and Legacy of
Rev. B. Lazarus and Sundaramma

Lazarus, B. - village preacher, evangelist, and church leader, was born (c. 1915) and raised in Devuni Padkal village, Thalakonda Pally Mandal, Ranga Reddy district, Telangana State, India. Lazarus had his schooling in the MB mission school, Shamshabad.

On the other hand, Sundaramma, preacher, evangelist, and women leader, was born in 1922[34] Keshampet village to Chennaiah and Ramulamma Koppu. She studied up to the third Forum at MB Mission School, Shamshabad, in 1932.

On 9 March 1942, Lazarus and Sundaramma's marriage was solemnised by Rev. J.J. Dick in Papireddy Gudem village. They were blessed with four sons and four daughters.

After their marriage, both Lazarus and Sundaramma had a theological education. Having graduated from the seminary, they proclaimed the Gospel in the villages of the Shamshabad Field. They preached the gospel in Eljarla, Solipet, Gaganpahad villages, etc. In 1951, they became preachers at Penjarla village, Kothur, Rangareddy district, and remained until their death.

Lazarus *panthulu* served in a variety of ministerial capacities in the Shamshabad Field. Throughout his ministry, Lazarus stood as a voice for the voiceless, equipping and empowering villagers, particularly

---

[34] B. Lazarus, "Suvarthannu Paadina Sundaramma" [Sundaramma who sang the gospel] *Suvarthamani* 69/8 (August 1992): 33.

believers, to trust in the transformational power of God. His life and ministry touched hundreds of lives across the Shamshabad Field. He was also known for his deep passion for evangelism.

In the 1980s, Lazarus was ordained by the MB Conference. Lazarus *panthulu* was passionate about winning souls for Christ. He was best known for his Christian Pastor's message of God's love.

On the other hand, Sundaramma *panthulamma* was a courageous woman minister. She boldly preached the message of salvation in Penjarla and nearby villages. Sundaramma was a gifted singer. Her interest was singing. She preached the good news of Jesus in the form of folk songs. It was easy for the villagers to understand, learn, and follow. Moreover, she gave more importance to personal evangelism. Consequently, many women embraced the Christian faith.

The role and contribution of Sundaramma *panthulamma* to enhancing women's ministry at the local, field, and conference levels are outstanding. She held different positions in the MB Field Women Association Shamshabad until she died in 1992. She encouraged women to learn Christian songs in the MB Women Field Association Shamshabad annual spiritual gatherings, MB Women Conference, or other women's meetings. She taught them singing.

Besides evangelism, Lazarus *panthulu* and Sundaramma *panthulamma* had a deep passion for empowering the poor and needy, including children, youth, and adults (men and women).[35] Therefore, they imparted education to them.

Lazarus *panthulu* and Sundaramma *panthulamma*

---

[35] Interview with B.L. Lemuel, Pastor and Chairman of MB Church Penjarla, 20 May 2021.

selflessly served in the villages throughout their ministry until they went to be with the heavenly father. On 9 June 1992, around 4 PM, Sundaramma *panthulamma* died in the MB Medical Center, Jadcherla, Mahabubnagar district.

2.23.

The Life and Legacy of
Mrs. B.P. Padma (1936-2016)

Padma Bootham Papaiah "B.P. Padma" – an educator, teacher, social worker, and woman leader, was born on 28 November 1936[36] to Papaiah and Mariamma Bootham in Shivannagudem village, of Devarakonda MB Field, Nalgonda district. On 3 May 1960, B.P. Padma married A.S. Caleb, eldest son of Sayanna and Kistamma Abbi, Papireddy Gudem village, near Shadnagar, Ranga Reddy district. Rev. V.L. Benjamin solemnised their holy matrimony. Caleb and Padma were blessed with a son, Daniel (wife – Anitha), and three daughters – Mercy (husband – Jaypaul), Esther Rani (husband – Paul), and Blessy Beulah (husband – Sunil Kumar).

Padma had her schooling at MB Mission School Shamshabad. Later, she worked in the same school. On 18 June 1952, she began her service as a teacher at MB School Shamshabad. In 1964, Padma became headmistress and Correspondent of the school. She retired in 1994. Since her retirement, Padma served as the school's correspondent until she died on 9 September 2015.

During her leadership, the school obtained Government grants-in-aid. It was upgraded into a high school by 1968 on an indigenous basis. Accordingly, the school became a full-fledged, co-educational, and

---

[36] Interview with A.C. Daniel, son of Mr. and Mrs. A.S. Caleb and Journalist, Shamshabad, 20 January 2021.

government-aided high school in that area, catering to the needs of the young minds today. It was the first of seven MB Schools recognised by the Government of Andhra Pradesh. Indeed, her contribution to educational work is commendable.

From the beginning of the history of Christianity in India, religious education has taken a central place in people's lives. Christian education is the systematic, definite teaching ministry of the Christian community. It helps its members become agents of transformation in and outside the community in their faith formation. Through the years, MB schools in general, MB High School Shamshabad in particular, under the leadership of B.P. Padma, continued to contribute to the Christian education programme of the Church to a greater or lesser extent. As a result, the literacy rate among young people increased.

Padma was also a prominent women leader in the MB Church in India. She worked for the cause of women's upliftment and social mobility. Her spirit of enthusiasm and dedication left a significant impact on many families, youth, and society.

Padma and her husband, Caleb, were outstanding local workers. They dedicated their lives to the development of MB School Shamshabad with a mission: 'Christian School is a step but not a stop into the church.'[37]

---

[37] A.S. David, "Ki.she A.S. Caleb gaari kluptha jeevitha charithra" [Brief biography of late A.S. Caleb], manuscript, Shamshabad, 2001.

2.24.
The Life and Legacy of
Rev. K.E. Paul (d. 1976)

Paul K.E. – Bible and school teacher, evangelist, pastor, and humanitarian, was born to Mrs. and Mr. Kondru Eedaiah in Ibrahimpatnam.[38] He married Ruthamma. She died in 1936. After two years, Paul married Lourence (Larinamma) in 1936. He was blessed with a daughter and two sons. In 1976, Paul died of cardiac arrest.

An MB local worker in the Ibrahimpatnam area motivated Paul to study at the MB mission school Shamshabad. Accordingly, Paul had his middle school education at Shamshabad and higher education at Methodist School Hyderabad. He also studied theology at MB Bible School Shamshabad.

He was fluent in the English language. Paul was an outstanding English teacher.[39] He opened a village school in Shabad village. All communities learned from him, irrespective of caste, creed, and status.

As teachers in the Bible School, local workers also played a significant role in bringing about social change in Society. Paul was a Bible teacher and taught several courses, including 'Theology,' 'Church History,' and 'Acts and Epistles' at MB Bible Institute Shamshabad.

In 1934, Paul and Ruthamma were appointed village

---

[38] Beracah MB Church Shabad, *Beracah MB Sangha Charithra Shabad mariyu Ki.She. K.E. Paul Gaari Charithra. Vajrothsava Vedukalu* [History of MB church Shabad and history of late K.E. Paul. Diamond jubilee] (Shabad: Beracah MB Church Shabad, 2011), 1-8.
[39] *India Mission Reports 1938-1970.* CMBS/Winnipeg, Canada.

preachers in Shabad village, 35 kilometres from MB mission station Shamshabad. Despite the hostility, they preached the gospel in Shabad and surrounding villages and led many people to Christ. Soon, they organised an MB Congregation in Shabad. They had regular worship services in a hut.

In 1936, his wife, Ruthamma, called to glory. In 1938, Paul married Lourence and moved to Shamshabad. However, in 1940, at the request of the elders of MB Church Shabad village, Paul and Lourence returned to Shabad and continued their service until they received the heavenly call.

In 1966, Paul began a church construction in Shabad. On 21 January 1971, the new church building was dedicated with the help of GC. Paul named the church after 'Beracah Mennonite Brethren Church.' Beracah ('Valley of Blessings') is mentioned in 2 Chronicles 20: 26 in the Hebrew Bible (Old Testament).

After the demise of K.E. Paul, his wife Lourence continued the ministry there until her death on 21 October 2001. Ruthamma was also active among local, field, and conference women.

Paul *panthulu* served as chairman of MB Field Association Shamshabad and contributed to the development of the Field. He was also an active social worker. For instance, he played a significant role in digging a drinking water well for Dalits in their colony. Paul, Ruthamma, and Lourence invested their lives to evangelize and uplift the Shabad area.

2.25.
The Life and Legacy of
G.J. Prabhavathi (1955 - 2021)

Prabhavathi Devapriyam – Bible Teacher, lyrist, gospel singer, and woman leader, was born on 10 April 1955[40] in the MB Mission Compound, Devarakonda, Nalgonda district, Telangana State, to Jacob and Meramma Gokamalla, of Rachoor village, Kalwakurthy, Nagarkurnool district. Prabhavathi was the eldest child in the family. She had two brothers and a sister: Timothy, Dinaker, and Hannamma. Her family moved to the MB Mission Compound Shamshabad, Ranga Reddy district, to assist MB missionaries and live the remainder of their lives.

Prabhavathi married R.S. Devapriyam, the eldest son of Samson and Yellamma Rachamalla of Shamshabad. God blessed them with Praveen, Susan Mary, and Betty Monica. On Saturday, 25 September 2021, due to cardiac arrest, Prabhavathi died at NIMS Hospital, Hyderabad,

She had schooling at MB Mission School Shamshabad (1 to 8 standards) and MB Central High School Mahabubnagar (9-10 classes and Intermediate). Prabhavathi earned a Bachelor of Theology degree at Andhra Christian Theological College (ACTC), Secunderabad, a Bachelor of Divinity degree (at ACTC), Secunderabad, from Senate of Serampore University, Kolkata, and a Master of Arts (Philosophy) from Osmania University, Hyderabad. Also, Prabhavathi, in

---

[40] Interview with R.D. Praveen, son of G.J. Prabhavathi, Shamshabad, 30 September 2021.

1976, enrolled in a Theological Course at MB Bible Institute Shamshabad and completed it successfully.

B.P. Padma, headmistress of the MB Mission School Shamshabad, and Rev. V.K. Rufus, principal of MBBI, impacted her spiritual life. During her schooling at Shamshabad, Prabhavathi was baptised by Rev. N.P. James at Bethany MB Church Shamshabad. Since then, she has become a communicant member of the Church. Prabhavathi served in different capacities in the local Church as a Sunday school teacher, Choir Director, woman leader, etc.

Prabhavathi was a multi-talented woman who served as a Bible Teacher, music teacher, typist (Telugu and English), and an instructor at MB Bible Institute, Shamshabad, from 1982 to 2005. Her contributions to empowering trainee pastors and evangelists at MBBI are noteworthy, for she taught worship songs, Telugu language (how to read and write to illiterate women), tailoring, and embroidery.

Prabhavathi held different positions in the MB Field Women Association Shamshabad, such as chairman, secretary, member, etc. Prabhavathi also actively organised a one-day or a four-day MB Field Women Spiritual Revival Meetings in the villages of Shamshabad Field. She also played a vital role in organizing the MB Girls camps among MB Churches in India.

For several years, Prabhavathi also served as an editorial board member for *Suvarthamani*, an official organ of MB Church of India (GC). She was a gifted writer. She penned several articles in the *Suvarthamani* for the spiritual edification of the believers, leaders, and youth. In addition, she wrote several worship songs in the Telugu language. Her songs are popular among MB Congregations and other Christian congregations. Some songs are:

hathasaakshulu chindinchina raktham –
kraisthava sanghanikade vitthanam
Vaaru chesina thyaaga phalitham –
sanghabhivruddhi kaade kaaranam

and

aadi sanghanaayakulanu – anusarinchudam eelalo
Amarula Jeevitha vidhaaname – manaku aadarshamaargamu

She worked in the Vishwa Vani Radio Ministries, Hyderabad, under Rev. Acharya R.R.K. Murthy. Prabhavathi's life reflects her completeness message as she balances ministry responsibilities with her duties as a wife to Devapriyam, mother of three, and proud grandmother. She was a woman with a passion for serving the Church and society.

Her husband, Rachamalla Devapriyam, also played a significant role in the MB Conference (GC), MB Field Shamshabad, and Bethany MB Church Shamshabad. Devapriyam died on 23 March 2013 in Shamshabad.

2.26.
The Life and Legacy of
G.Y. Prabhudas (1952-2013)

Prabhudas G.Y. – Layman and Agricultural Officer, was born on 13 June 1952 to G.P. Yesurathnam (Ushaiah) and Ramulamma in Shamshabad.[41] He was the first child in the family. On 9 May 1975, Prabhudas married N. Padma. They were blessed with G.P. Stephen, G.P. Paulson, G.P. Blessington, and G.P. Elizabeth Rani. Prabhudas died on 16 April 2013 at Care Hospital, Banjara Hills, Hyderabad, around 12:10 am.

Prabhudas had his pre-primary schooling at MB High School Shamshabad. Then, he went to the *Zilla Parishath* High School (ZPHS) for primary and high school. Prabhudas was one of the students of the First SSC Batch (Tenth class, English Medium) 1969. From 1970 to 1972, he studied Intermediate at Mehboob College, Secunderabad. Prabhudas earned a Bachelor of Arts degree in 1975 and a Master of Arts (Public Administration) from Osmania University, Hyderabad, in 1981. He also earned a Bachelor of Science (Agriculture) from Acharya N.G. Ranga Agricultural University), Hyderabad, in 1990 (now known as Professor Jayashankar Telangana State Agricultural University).

Prabhudas was a youth leader in the MB Central Youth (GC) and MB Field Youth Association Shamshabad. As a youth leader, he inspired many young

---

41 Interview with G.P. Padma, Chairman of the Bethany MB Women Fellowship, Shamshabad, 2 October 2021.

men and women. Prabhudas was also a member of the MB Board of Theological Education (GC), CRC (Committee of Reference and Counsel), and MB Convention Committee. He played a significant role in evangelizing in Shamshabad Field. He served as a member, treasurer, secretary, vice-chairman, or Acting Chairman of the MB Field Association for several years. The GC commissioned Prabhudas at MB Church Gaganpahad.

Prabhudas served as the Chairman of the Bethany MB Church Shamshabad for several years. He also served as the Pastor of MB Church Maheshwaram. Furthermore, he was essential in constructing church buildings at Tadiparthy and Yacharam villages.

Besides church ministry, as an agricultural officer, he always helped the needy and poor farmers. He toured several villages to enlighten farmers with agricultural science. In 1977, he joined as a Village Extension Officer (VEO) in the Agricultural Department and retired on 30 June 2010. The VEO is the key component of the agriculture sector after a farmer; one of the VEO's primary duties is keeping farmers up to date with modern and advanced farming knowledge and techniques. Consequently, it will upsurge the efficiency of agricultural produce.

Prabhudas served as the President of the Gandhi Youth Club and empowered youth. Prabhudas' contributions to the Church and society are highly appreciated.

2.27.

The Life and Legacy of
Rev. P.J. Prakasham (1935-2006)

Prakasham P. J. – preacher and evangelist, was born on 24 November 1935[42] in Bijaram village, Dhanwada Mandal, Narayanpet district, Telangana State. His parents, Jacob and Esther, worked as gardeners in the MB Mission Compound, Narayanpet.

Being born into a Hindu family, he was strongly influenced by Arya Samaj's teachings. From his childhood, Prakasham was against Christianity and its teachings. Consequently, he strongly opposed conversion to Christianity. Several times, he opposed MB missionaries visiting the village.

However, a gospel tract entitled "Jesus Came to Save the Sinners" (Luke 5:32) turned his life. Prakasham wanted to know who Jesus Christ was. MB missionaries explained that Jesus came to seek and save the sinners and gave HIS life on the cross. He accepted Jesus Christ and was baptized in 1948.

In 1952, he married Rathnamma at MB Mission Compound, Wanaparthy. They had seven children: Deborah, Suryakantha, Abigala, Peterbabu, Esther, Sarala, and Emmanuel.

Prakasham was influenced by Rev. Dan Nickel, MB missionary, who washed the feet of a village believer in Church worship. He began to work with Dan Nickel in the Narayanpet area. A bicycle was his means of

---

[42] Interview with David Talwar, pastor - MB Field Narayanpet, Shamshabad, 30 June 2021.

transport. He always carried a lamp as he traveled through a forest in the evenings. He was attacked by a leopard one day, but God saved him.

Prakasham served as Pastor of MB Church Singaram and MB Church Narayanpet. With the help of his family members, he constructed a church building in Singaram village. He solemnized hundreds of marriages.

Prakasham encouraged villagers to send their children to school. He taught the poor and downtrodden children and sent them to the MB mission hostel, Narayanpet.

Prakasham also encouraged youth to become involved in ministry. He encouraged many young men to study theology. He served in the MB Conference and MB Field Narayanpet in different positions for several years.

Prakasham received high respect from people irrespective of caste and creed for his humility and service. On 24 March 2006, Prakasham died suddenly in a hospital.

2.28.

The Life and Legacy of
Rev. R. Praveen Kumar (1973-2021)

P raveen Kumar – evangelist, pastor, and writer, was born on March 02, 1973, to R. Timothy and P.A. Helen in Kurnool, Andhra Pradesh. He married Sharon Rose, eldest daughter of Rev. P.A. John and Mrs. Hemalatha John, Wanaparthy, on 13 October 1997, at Olive MB Church, Wanaparthy.[43] Rev. R.S. Lemuel solemnised their marriage. He also delivered the wedding sermon. They were blessed with a daughter – Thabitha, and a son – Timothy. Praveen Kumar went home to be with the Lord on Thursday early hours, 13 May 2021, in the Government Hospital Wanaparthy, due to COVID-19 complications.

Praveen Kumar earned several degrees - a Bachelor of Arts from STBC College, Kurnool, a Bachelor of Theology degree at MBC Bible College, Shamshabad (1994-1998), and a Bachelor of Divinity degree at Andhra Christian Theological College, Secunderabad, in 2019 from the Senate of Serampore College (University).

From 1998 to 2003, while serving as the Pastor of MB Church, Kurnool, he also evangelised in five villages. On 27 July 2003, he became the MB Warkentin Memorial Church pastor, Kalwakurthy, Nagarkurnool district, Telangana State. He faithfully served as their beloved pastor for 17 years, i.e., until 30 April 2018. Praveen Kumar loved his church members dearly and

---

[43] Interview with R.P. Timothy, son of Rev. R. Praveen Kumar, on the phone, 23 May 2021.

compassionately and always felt it a privilege and a joy to pastor the flock. He is popularly known as 'Kalwakurthy Praveen.' During that time, he also served as the chairman of the Church. On May 1, 2018, he was appointed pastor of the Centenary MB Church, MB Medical Center, Kaveramma Peta, Jadcherla. Since then, he served as the pastor there until he went to be with the Heavenly Father in May 2021. Praveen Kumar was a practical preacher of the Word of God with a message of hope and salvation. He won many disciples for Christ.

Praveen Kumar worked in the MB Conference of India in several different capacities over the years. He served as the MB Board of Evangelism and Church Ministries (GC) Secretary. As the secretary, Praveen Kumar visited several MB Churches across India. He encouraged MB pastors, church elders, believers, and youth to expand His Kingdom. Praveen Kumar served as one of the Editorial Board of Suvarthamani members for over a decade. He also served as the editor of *Suvarthamani* from 2016 to 2021.[44] Moreover, Praveen Kumar, a member of the Donor Council of the MB Centenary Bible College, Shamshabad, recurrently contributed to the College.

Besides evangelism, he also engaged in philanthropic services. He supported pastors and evangelists regularly. Praveen Kumar received respect from believers, pastors, and evangelists.

---

[44] Yennamalla Jayaker, "Obituary of Rev. R. Praveen Kumar (1973-2021)," printed script, Shamshabad, 13 May 2021.

2.29.
The Life and Legacy of
Rev. Bhoompag Aaron Ross and
Sharamma

Ross Aaron Bhoompag "B.A. Ross" – Freedom Fighter, humanitarian, churchman, musician, translator, pastor, and evangelist, was born to Rev. Bhoompag Aaron and Mrs. Rose Manikyamma, the first converts to Christianity in the Gadwal Field, on 27 August 1927. Rev. Bhoompag Aaron founded MB Mizpah Church, Gadwal, and many more churches. Ross was the oldest of eleven children.

In 1959, Ross married Sharamma, the eldest daughter of Rev. M. Isaiah and M. Ketamma. Ross and Sharamma had six sons and four daughters – B. Shulamithi Ross, B. Bealiah Ross, B. Johanna Ross, B. John Ross, B. Salomi Ross, Late B. Mary Pramila Kumari, B. Abraham Ross, B. Jacob Ross, Late B. Silus Ross, and Rev. B. Roser Benhur Ross.[45]

Ross and Sharamma had their Biblical studies at Ramayapatnam. Ross received the heavenly call on 16 October 2006. "On his funeral day, the gathering witnessed a rare phenomenon: a dove stopped in the air for a few minutes and hovered over his mortal remains. Many onlookers took it as a sign that he was God's well-beloved," says B. Jacob Ross.[46]

Ross started his education at the Government Boys

---

[45] Interview with B. Roser Benhur Ross, younger son of Rev. B.A. Ross, Gadwal, 20 December 2021.

[46] B. Jacob Ross, "Biography of Bhoompag Aron Ross," Typescript, December 2021.

High School, Gadwal. He pursued higher education at Hislop Degree College, Nagpur. He also had a Teacher's Training.

Ross served as a clerk in the Government Tahsil Office, Gadwal. Later, he worked as a teacher. B. Jacob Ross says, "The Queen of Gadwal, Maharani Adi Laxmi Devamma, appointed him a teacher. He was elevated to Headmaster and retired as Inspector of Schools. Ross's students include Mr. D.K. Samarasimha Reddy, a former minister, D.K. Bharatha Simha Reddy, a former MLA, and many more."[47]

He was a lover of languages. Ross fluently spoke Telugu, Hindi, English, Urdu, Marathi, and Kannada. He also learned Hebrew and Greek. A Polyglot!

Ross was popularly known by the sobriquet 'Coat Sir.' Because his attire was always white: white trousers, a white shirt, teamed with a black blazer.

Ross was a man of prayer, a keen listener, a wise advisor, hardworking, disciplined, a translator, and a musician. The obedient parents dedicated their firstborn, Ross, to the service of the Lord. Accordingly, Ross educated himself in theological studies at Union Biblical Seminary, Yavatmal, Maharashtra. Enlightened, he vehemently defended the right doctrine against the cult.

Ross was very conservative, following the doctrines of the Mennonites in letter and spirit. He opposed the doctrines of the Bible fervently. Ross openly criticized the wrong doctrines and cults in society.

He carved a niche for himself as a speaker with excellent communication skills for the masses and educated. He devoted his life to preaching and teaching. Preaching was in his blood. His love for the word of God

---

[47] Ross, "Biography of Bhoompag Aron Ross."

gave him the titles 'Walking Bible' and 'Repository of the Bible.' He did not need to open the Bible to look for any reference. Every verse was on the tip of his tongue. Ross had the zeal to carry the Word of God to his people.

Ross was one of the founding members of the MB Field Youth Association, Gadwal. He believed that youth have a more significant impact on the church and society. He assisted missionaries in language learning and ministry.

He was also determined to show God's love to the community. Ross shepherded the MB Mizpah Church for more than 20 years. He pastored the Melachruvu church, Olive MB Church, and Gadwal for many years. Ross was a prolific preacher with an indelible impression that voice was powerful. His messages would grip the congregation. Ross led many thousands to receive the Lord Jesus as his personal Saviour.

Gadwal is a historical place ruled by Maharani Adi Laxmi Devamma. It is famous for *Jatara* (fair), a festival organized in honour of local go, celebrated from time unknown. *Chinna Jatara* and *Pedda Jatara* are times of fun and gaiety. People from the surrounding villages exhibit their craft from various walks of life. Ross availed this opportunity to speak with the people of other faiths. He used to set up a stall and distribute pamphlets and tracts about the 'Plan of Redemption.' Ross used a *Boora* (a wind instrument, a kind of Natural Horn) to trumpet the Gospel in villages. He also did tremendous work in Bombay, Raichur, and Gangavathi.

Ross and Sharamma travelled extensively to several villages or towns with the message of salvation. They endured all sorts of hardships in the ministry.

Ross was a man of faith. He trusted the Lord for all his needs throughout his life. "It is better to trust in the

LORD than to put confidence in man," Ps 118:8 was his life motto. Even for a pencil, he taught his children to look to God. The Lord honoured his faith and provided all his needs. The Lord Almighty used him as His Chosen vessel to enrich and enhance the spiritual life of many.

Ross served in several capacities in the MB Conference India (GC), MB Board of Evangelism, the Gadwal Field Association, and MB Mizpah Church. He also rendered his services to the Bible Society of India.

Ross and Sharamma were very generous in hospitality to the poor and the needy, irrespective of caste, creed, and status. Ross was highly regarded in society, for he maintained a cordial relationship with all communities.

Furthermore, Ross had extensive knowledge of *Ayurveda* and Allopathy medicines. He voluntarily helped the sick. Ross established Grace MPHW Training Institute[48] to train girls from humble backgrounds, thus providing self-sustenance. Whenever he found people in trouble, he supported and aided them with anything possible.

In and around Gadwal, many families recall a facet of Ross' life where he never missed attending any funeral and comforted the bereaved family. Ross always carried the Holy Bible, even to his workplace. Once, a collector asked him, "Why do you always carry a Bible?" Ross reciprocated that the 'Bible is the Universal Constitution.'

His love was not only for the God he worshipped but

---

[48] Multi-purpose Health Worker (MPHW) is a medical level course during which the males and females are trained to handle and perform health care activities. This course is designed to prepare the candidates for multiple works like emergency health care services at lower levels in various places.

also for his country. Ross had a great affinity for the land where he lived, India. He participated in the Indian Independence Struggle and was a proud recipient of the 'Jewel of India Award.'

Ross's fervour and passion for the Lord and lost souls were contagious and convincing. He was dedicated to passionately pursuing God's calling in his life. Ross and Sharamma's lives reflect the total devotion to the Lord Christ and the Gospel's message.

Their children are carrying forward the legacy left behind by this towering personality.

2.30.

The Life and Legacy of
Rev. V.K. Rufus (1942-2003)

Rufus Vedulla "V.K. Rufus" – Churchman, pastor, administrator, and theologian, was born on 9 June 1942, in Arutla village, Ibrahimpatnam Mandal, Ranga Reddy district, Telangana State, India, to Kanakaiah and Sathyamma Vedulla. He was the third child of two daughters and two sons. Rufus lost his father when he was five years old.

On 22 May 1974,[49] Rufus married Milka Virginia Devakrupa at Bethany Mennonite Brethren Church (Shamshabad). Rufus and Virginia Vedulla were blessed with one daughter and two sons. Rufus died on June 7, 2003, in Shamshabad.

From 1974 to 2003, Rufus and Virginia lived in Shamshabad, where Rufus was instrumental in enhancing theological education, reaching unreached villages of the Shamshabad area, and leading many people to Christ. Moreover, he was decisive in establishing the MB Historical Archive in Shamshabad in the early 1980s. Virginia Rufus served as a teacher in the MB High School, Shamshabad. She also played a significant role among women.

Rufus had his early education in his home village, Arutla. Later, Rufus had his schooling at MB Mission Schools at Shamshabad (1952-53), at Hughestown (fourth to seventh standards), at Mahabubnagar (Tenth

---

[49] Interview with Dennis Vedulla, younger son of Rev. V.K. Rufus, Shamshabad, 18 October 2018.

and eleventh standards), and the Government School, Zamistanpur, Hyderabad (Eight and ninth standards). While Rufus attended the MB Mission School (Hughestown), he was baptised on December 2, 1957, at Bethel MB Church, Hughestown, by Rev. D. Franz Joshua.

Rufus earned several degrees – a one-year theological certificate course from Bethany Bible School, Shamshabad in 1961, a G.Th. from Ramayapatnam Baptist Theological Seminary (1961-1965), a BA degree from Tabor College, Hillsboro, Kansas, USA, in 1972, an MA degree in Christian Education from North American Baptist Seminary (USA) in 1973, and an M.Div. and a Th.M. degree from Fuller Theological Seminary and Trinity Evangelical Divinity School, USA (1989-1992).[50]

Rufus was a communicant member of Bethel MB Church, Hughestown, from 1957 to 1966. Later, in 1966, he joined Bethany MB Church, Shamshabad, and remained with that Church until he died in 2003.

He served in the MB Conference of India in several different capacities. Rufus, at other times, served as Bible Teacher (1965-2003), Registrar, Bursar, and Principal (1980-1989, 1993-2003) of the Mennonite Brethren Bible School/College (Shamshabad). Rufus served as the first national Director of Mennonite Brethren Christian Education (1973-1980). He served as a vice-president of the Governing Council of the Conference of Mennonite Brethren Churches of India (GC) (1998-2002), Treasurer (GC), chairman of Mennonite Brethren Board of Evangelism and Church Ministries (GC), Mennonite

---

[50] Solomon, E.D., comp., "60 Samvathsaraala Devuni Krupalo Rev. V. K. Rufus (1942 -)" [60 Years of God's Grace: Rev. V. K. Rufus (1942 -)] (Shamshabad: MBCBC & BMBC, 2003).

Brethren Board of Education, Committee of Reference and Counsel and Mennonite Brethren Field Association Shamshabad. Rufus also served as the pastor and chairman of Bethany MB Church, Shamshabad (1987-1989 and 2002-2003). In addition, Rufus actively participated in the Mennonite Christian Service Fellowship of India (MCSFI), Andhra Pradesh Christian Council (APCC), and Mennonite World Conference.

Rufus attended as a delegate at several international conferences, such as the AMB Centenary celebrations in Brazil and Reedley (USA) in 1984, the Asian Mennonite Conference in Taiwan in 1985, the International Committee of Mennonite Brethren in Kansas, USA, in 1999, and Mennonite World Conference in Winnipeg in 1981. Rufus also visited Singapore, Germany, and France.

On December 9, 1987, Rufus was ordained as a minister of the Word of God by the MB Conference of India (GC) in Bethany MB Church, Shamshabad.[51]

Rufus wrote two theses on the historical foundations of the Mennonite Brethren Church in India:

i) "Strangers in Karnataka: Mennonite Brethren Historical Foundations." M.Div. thesis, Fuller Theological Seminary, USA, April 1992.

ii) "Strangers in Maharashtra: Mennonite Brethren Historical Foundations." Th.M. thesis, Trinity Evangelical Divinity School, USA, December 1992.

Rufus was instrumental in establishing Sunday schools and conducting training programmes for Sunday school teachers. Rufus encouraged and challenged people to become ministers and laid a strong foundation

---

[51] Interview with Vedulla.

for pastoral ministry. Although Rufus was highly educated, he kept a model of simplicity and workmanship. Punctuality, honesty, and discipline were Rufus's code words. He stood as a role model of Christ and did not fear death. Until his last breath, he served the Lord. Memories of Rufus's sacrificial work remain in people's hearts.

2.31.
The Life and Legacy of
Rev. E.M. Samuel (1947-2014)

Samuel Eerlapally "E.M. Samuel" – village preacher, evangelist, and Churchman, was born in 1947[52] in Gafoornagar (Thulasinagar) village, Kandukur Mandal, Rangareddy district, Telangana State. His parents, Moses and Shiphoramma Eerlapally, were poor farmers and pioneer Christians. Samuel was the first in a family of two sons and four daughters. His siblings are – one brother, Yesurathnam (wife – Susheela), and four sisters – Devamma (husband – Mohan), Pushpamma (husband – Devasahayam), Premamma (husband – Eliah), and Sharamma (husband – Sudarshan K.).

In 1969, Samuel married Bharathamma, eldest daughter of Andraiah and Jangamma Jonnada, of Muchintal village, Shamshabad Mandal, Rangareddy district, at Mennonite MB Gafoornagar. Rev. K.E. Paul, the pastor of MB Church Shabad, solemnised their wedding. Samuel and Bharathamma were blessed with two sons and a daughter – Joseph (wife – Deepa), Joel (wife – Amulya), and Jayasheela (husband – Devaraj). On November 29, 2014,[53] Samuel died in his home village, Gafoornagar.

In 1966, Rev. Goneh Jonah, pastor of MB Church Maheshwaram, baptised E.M. Samuel at MB Church Gafoornagar. He remained a communicant member of

---

[52] Interview with K.S. Sharamma, youngest sister of Rev. E.M. Samuel, Shadnagar, 9 July 2020.

[53] Interview with E.S. Joseph, eldest son of Rev. E.M. Samuel, on the phone, Shamshabad, 9 July 2020.

the Church until his death.

Samuel had his primary education at MB Mission School Shamshabad. Later, he went to Mahabubnagar to pursue a high school education at MB High School. He completed his HSC in 1965. In 1970, Samuel and Bharathamma went to Shamshabad to pursue theological studies at MB Bethany Bible School. He completed a Certificate in Theology course.

Samuel served as pastor of the Calvary MB Church, Mankhal (1974-1997), Jonah MB Church, Maheshwaram village (1998 – 2003), MB Church, Shabad (2003 – 2005), and MB Church Gafoornagar (2005-2010).

On 15 December 2002, Samuel was ordained as a minister of the Word of God by the Mennonite Brethren Conference of India (GC) at MB Church Gafoornagar.

Samuel served in the MB Field Association of Shamshabad in various capacities at different periods, as chairman, vice-chairman, secretary, assistant secretary, treasurer, and member.

Samuel also served as a member of the MB Board of Evangelism and Church Ministries (GC) in 1999. Samuel and his wife, Bharathamma, attended as delegates to the Mennonite World Conference, held in Kolkata, India, in 1997.

Samuel served as a Christian Marriage Registrar with a Government Christian Marriage Licence to solemnise marriage(s) between Christians. In his pastoral ministry, he solemnised more than 100 Christian marriages.

Though he announced his voluntary retirement in 2011, he never gave up his passion for HIS mission work until he was called to glory in 2014. He encouraged and supported many evangelists and pastors, irrespective of denomination.

Samuel was a brilliant student in education. He always

aimed to be at the top of the schooling or theological institute class. Samuel learned the English language with enthusiasm and spoke English fluently.

Samuel was one of the local workers of MB Church. He played a significant role in spreading Christianity in villages of the Shamshabad Field Association. He also encouraged many parents to send their children to the village or mission school, Shamshabad. On 9 December 2014, at Samuel's Memorial Service, K. Asheervadam, Chairman – of Calvary MB Church Mankhal village, asserted, "Rev. E.M. Samuel is not only a priest but also an agent of social transformation. He believed education transforms the lives of subaltern people. He motivated my parents to send me to Hyderabad for higher education."[54]

Samuel committed himself to discipleship throughout his ministry, leaving an excellent legacy for the next generation.

---

[54] K. Asheervadam, "Tributes: Celebrating the Life of Rev. E.M. Samuel," Gafoornagar village, Kandukur Mandal, Ranga Reddy district, December 9, 2014.

2.32.

The Life and Legacy of
Rev. Sharada Arnold (1946-2017)

Sharada Arnold – a woman leader and administrator, was born on 14 July 1946 at Gangaram village, Nagarkurnool.[55] Her parents are pastor K. Enoch and Krupamma.

On 6 June 1966, Sharada married Dr. P.B. Arnold, son of Rev. P.B. Benjamin and Sharamma, of Gollapally village, Wanaparthy. Rev. P.B. Abraham solemnised the marriage at Gangaram village, Nagarkurnool. They had six children, five daughters and a son – Margaret Anuradha, Anupama Ruth, Veena, Manjeera, Shilpa, and Samuel Arun Kumar.

Sharada Arnold visited several countries, including the USA, Canada, the UK, Israel, Switzerland, Germany, Africa, Zimbabwe, Kenya, Israel, Holland, Japan, Taiwan, Thailand, etc. On 25 October 2017, at 5 pm, Sharada died at KIMS Hospital Hyderabad.

She studies at MB School (1 to 4 class) and Government High School (5 to 10 class) Mahabubnagar. Sharada earned a Bachelor of Arts from Osmania University, Hyderabad (at Reddy Women's College, Narayanguda, Hyderabad).

After Rev. Dr. P.B. Arnold was elected President of the MB Churches of India, Sharada was designated Honourable President of the MB Women's Fellowship. During the course of time, she effectively strengthened and organised it as the MB Women's Conference of

---

India. She persuaded the GC to recognise women's leadership and bestow on their positions in Churches, Field Associations, and GC Committees.

She served as the chairperson of the Centenary MB Church till 2017. Sharada's contribution to the management and administration of medical work was noteworthy.

In 2008, she was elected as one of the vice presidents of the MB Conference. Sharada was instrumental in obtaining unanimous approval for the Commissioning and Ordinations of Women leaders in the MB Conference of India. Accordingly, sixty women ministers were ordained for the ministry of the Word of God on 8 November 2008 at the Golden Jubilee celebrations of the Governing Council of the Conference of the MBCI, held in MB Mission Compound, Mahabubnagar.

Sharada was always ready to help the victims of natural disasters across India. She played a significant role in raising funds, food, and clothing for flood or tsunami-affected families.

Sharada emphasised women's empowerment. She played a key role in forming the MB *Krishtava Mahila Vikaasam*, a separate wing for the upliftment of women, which was started in 1987. Its first programme was a thrift shop called '*Pedala Pennidi*,'[56] to offer clothes for the poor, the needy, and widows. Sharada served the Conference faithfully and fearlessly till the last moment.

---

[56] Yennamalla Jayaker, "The Role of the Mennonite Brethren Church of India in the Upliftment of Telangana Region from 1958-2008" (Master of Theology thesis, Senate of Serampore College (University), 2011), 96.

2.33.

The Life and Legacy of
Rev. Sowlollu Solomon (1952 - 2008)

Solomon Sowlollu – theologian, pastor, and Churchman was born on January 7, 1952, to John Pothappa and Sundaramma Sowlollu in Nandavaram village, Kurnool district, Andhra Pradesh. He married Vasanthamma on April 23, 1971. They had two sons and three daughters: Rev. Samuel Prasad, Vijaya Gladys, Lilly Roselyn, Albert, and Shobha Sukasini. Solomon died on Saturday, March 01, 2008, at Temple University Hospital, PA., USA, at 57 years of age.[57]

Solomon studied SSLC at Zilla Parishath School, Nandavaram. He completed a Certificate of Theology at MB Bible Institute, Shamshabad. He earned a Bachelor of Theology (Union Biblical Seminary, Yeovatmal), a Bachelor of Divinity (Senate of Serampore College), a Master of Arts in Philosophy, and a Master of Arts of English Litt. (Osmania University, Hyderabad), a Master of Theology (Regent College, Vancouver), a Master of Philosophy of English Litt. (Madurai Kamaraj University), and a Conflict Transformation Programme (Eastern Mennonite University, USA).

Soloman worked as a warden at the Social Welfare Department, Nadavaram (1969-1971). He served as the Pastor of MB Church Yenugabala, Yemmiganur (1976), MB Church, Jadcherla (1980), MB Mizpah Church

---

[57] Interview with S. Samuel Prasad, Pastor of Bethany MB Church, Shamshabad, 10 September 2020.

Gadwal (1986-1991), and Bethany MB Church Shamshabad (1991-1992). From 1985 to 2008, he served at different MB Theological Institutions as registrar, principal, vice-principal, treasurer, and director of Peace Studies.

Solomon held different leadership positions in the MB Conference – as Chairman of, MB Field Association, Yemmiganur (1989-2008), Peace Committee (1997-1999), MB Hostels (1995-1997), Committee of Reference and Counsel (1997-2002), MB Board of Evangelism and Church Ministries (2002-2006), and MB Board of Education (2002-2005); vice-chairman of MB Field Association, Yemmiganur (1986-1989), and MCSFI (2003-2005); secretary (1995-2008) and treasurer of the GC (1989-1994); MB Board of Theological Education (1992-1993, 1997-1999, and 2003-2005), Committee of Reference and Counsel (CRC) (2002-2006); the member of MCSFI (1990-1996), Church Partnership Evangelism (1995-2008), Mission Committee (1995-2008), APCC, NCCI (2005-2008), Mennonite World Conference (2003-2009), editor of *Suvarthamani* - monthly magazine (2002-2005).

Solomon attended international Mennonite gatherings like the Mennonite World Conference (1990 and 2003) and the Asian Mennonite Conference (1992 and 1994). He visited several countries, including Nepal, Canada, USA, Hong Kong, Bangkok, Thailand, Indonesia, Singapore, Malaysia, Guatemala, Africa, South Africa, London, Germany, Amsterdam (Holland), Japan, Kuwait, Panama, Bangladesh, and Pakistan.

2.34.
The Life and Legacy of
Pastor Sri Katta Veeraiah

V eeraiah Sri Katta was born to Sri Katta Ramreddy and Rathnamma at Lingotam village, Achampet, Nagarkurnool district, Telangana State, India. Veeraiah married Manikyamma in 1926.[58] Mrs. Manikyamma died in 1930 due to a severe attack of cholera. Later, he married Karunamma, Kothakota, Wanaparthy in 1932. God blessed them with five children: four sons – Samuel, Leander, Sunder, Purushotham, and a daughter, Bhagyamma.

During an evangelical tour in 1966, he fell sick. He was admitted into MB Medical Center, Jadcherla. On November 14, 1966, Veeraiah died in the hospital.

In 1925, Veeraiah accepted the Lord Jesus Christ as his saviour and embraced Christianity. Pastor Talluri Ezra baptised him. Rev. D.F. Bergthold and Pastor Pulukuri Joseph were his spiritual mentos.

After completing a Bible Seminary course at Nagarkurnol, Veeraiah and Manikyamma worked as village preachers at Devuni Tirmalapuram. Manikyamma died in the same village.

Both Veeraiah and Karunamma continued their ministry as village preachers and evangelists in the villages of Devuni Tirmalapuram (1933-1941), Talupunur (1942-43), Uppununthala (1944-1948), and

---

[58] Interview with K.V. Purushotham, Treasurer GC, Nagarkurnool, March 4, 2021; "Late Sri Katta Veeraiaha and Smt. Karunamma," *MB Mission Centenary Celebrations Nagarkurnool (1904-2004). Souvenir* (Nagarkurnool: MB Church Nagarkurnool, 2004).

Gaddampalli (1949-166). Besides pastoral duties, he regularly had gospel tours.

He worked under Rev. J.N. Hiebert, Rev. J.J. Kasper, Rev. J.J. Dick, and Rev. A.A. Unruh. They always appreciated his hard work and passion for extending HIS Kingdom. After his death, his wife, Karunamma, continued the ministry at Gaddampalli for the remainder of her life.

Throughout his life, Veeraiah led a simple and exemplary life. Though he converted from a high-caste community, he never encouraged caste discrimination. Veeraiah reached the Dalits with the good news of Jesus Christ. He also imparted education to village children to bring about social transformation.

2.35.
The Life and Legacy of
G.Y. Vidyasagar (1956-2000)

Vidyasagar Pedda Gandu "G.Y. Vidyasagar" – social worker, politician, and evangelist was born on 19 December 1956 at the MB Missionary Hospital, Mission Compound, Shamshabad, Telangana State. He was the second child in the family. His parents were G.P. Yesurathnam (Ushaiah) and Venkatamma. On 23 December 1977,[59] he married Premalatha and was blessed with two sons, Prem Sagar and Pavithra Sagar, and three daughters, Snehalatha, Srilatha, and Vidyulatha. On 22 April 2000, Vidyasagar died in a car accident at Palamakula village, near Shamshabad.

Vidyasagar had his primary schooling at Boys High School Shamshabad. He studied from the eighth standard to the Intermediate at Government High School, Kachiguda, Hyderabad. He earned a Bachelor of Arts degree. After his education, Vidyasagar assisted his father in the agricultural field and road contract work.

Vidyasagar was passionate about sharing the gospel with the unreached from his childhood. He learned about the Bible and evangelism from Ezra panthulu, Shamshabad for three years. He read English Newspapers and listened to English News on the Radio to speak English fluently. Consequently, he worked as a translator to missionaries in rural evangelism for several years. In addition, he learned the *Lambada* (*Banjara*) language to reach the *Banjara* Tribal people.

---

[59] Interview with G.V. Premalatha, wife of G.Y. Vidyasagar, Shamshabad, 30 September 2021.

Vidyasagar also regularly visited several villages with the good news of Jesus and led many villagers to Christ. In 1991, he was blessed with a two-wheeler (Scooter), on which Vidyasagar travelled over a hundred kilometres to preach the gospel. His main aim was to reach the unreached with the saving knowledge of Jesus Christ. Vidyasagar toured several villages, including Shapur, Muchinthala, Burjugadda Tanda, Koduru, Ummethala, Raikal, Ghanapur, Annaram, Burgula, Bharathnagar Colony, and so on. He always loved the needy, the poor, and the helpless.

Vidyasagar worked with an outstanding commitment among the lepers in the Leprosy Colony, near Railway Station Shamshabad (Umdanagar). He worked as a warden of the MB Mission Hostel, Mission Compound Shamshabad, for over five years, starting in 1987. Vidyasagar spiritually led hostellers. On Good Friday, 21 April 2000, he preached his last sermon at the MB Church in Muchintala village. He preached the fourth statement of Jesus from the cross, "My God, My God, Why Have You Forsaken Me?" (Mark 15: 34). On the same evening, he attended a wedding with P. Indra Reddy, a politician. On 22 April 2000, while returning from the wedding party, their car met with an accident on the National Highway 44 at Palamakula village around 12:30 a.m. Vidyasagar, P. Indra Reddy, and the car driver were killed.

Besides evangelism, Vidyasagar was very active in politics. He was a member of the Congress Party, Gandhi Bhavan, since 1978. In 1994, he was appointed a Convenor of the Ranga Reddy District Congress Committee Scheduled Caste/Scheduled Tribes (SC/ST) Cell. From 1995 to 1999, he oversaw the Congress Party Shamshabad. In 1995, Vidyasagar was appointed SC Cell

Secretary Andhra Pradesh State (Pradesh Congress Committee). In 1996, he was appointed Organising Secretary of Ranga Reddy District Congress Committee.

From 1981 to 1986, he served as a Ward Member of Grama Panchayati Shamshabad. Vidyasagar also worked as a Co-option member of the Primary Agricultural Credit Society (PACS) for many years. Furthermore, in 1993, he was appointed General Secretary of Scheduled Castes United Front Ranga Reddy district, Andhra Pradesh.

Vidyasagar had a healthy relationship with the then State Ministers, Member(s) of Parliament (MPs), Members(s) of the Legislative Assembly (MLAs), other political leaders, and public servants. He visited Delhi several times. With the influence of the leaders, Vidyasagar helped the poor and downtrodden people with economic upliftment projects. Consequently, many received Tractors for their agriculture. Through his efforts, many homeless people got homes or land from the Government.

Moreover, Vidyasagar played a significant role in the 'Telangana Movement for a Separate State,' which began in the 1950s. The people of the Telangana region started organising themselves under various organisations with a demand for a separate State of Telangana. Several times, Vidyasagar was imprisoned for participating in the movement. Several cases were filed against him.

Besides evangelism, he focused on philanthropic works to uplift the poor and downtrodden people. In short, he reflected Christ's love in action.

2.36.
The Life and Legacy of
Rev. P.S. Zacharaiah (1929-1997)

Zachariah P.S. – evangelist and pastor, was born to P. Sayanna and Eedamma (Lizamma) in 1929 at Kalwakurthty, Nagarkurnool district, Telangana State, India. He married Navamma, daughter of B. Abraham, and Sharamma of Midgil village near Kalwakurthy. Her parents were the first believers in Midgil.

On 29 February 1948, P.V. Henry and G. Jeevarathnam baptised him. He had theological training at MB Bible School, Devarakonda, from 1949 to 1951. From 1951-52, he worked as a lecturer at the MB Elementary Bible School Narayanpet. Later, on November 25, 1952,[60] he was appointed Pastor of MB Bethany Church, Kalwakurthy. He remained there until he died on January 5, 1997.

He received commissioning in 1955 and ordination in 1963. He worked with MB missionaries – J.A. Wiebe, J.H. Lohrenz, Ted Fast, D.A. Nickel, Henry Poetker, and others to extend MB church in the Kalwakurthy area.

He played a significant role in reaching several villages with the good news of Jesus Christ. He used to tour villages on a bicycle. He preached the gospel in several villages, including Panjugulla, Thurkalapally, Lingareddy Pally, Kotra, Thandra, Jupally, Charakonda, Raghupathipet, Ramagiri, Midjil, Kondareddypally,

---

[60] P.Z. Wilson, "Brief History of Late Rev. P.S. Zacharaiah (1929-1997)," in *The Golden Jubilee Celebrations of the Governing Council of the Conference of the Mennonite Brethren Church of India* (Mahbubnagar: MBCI, 2009).

Zakinapally, Venkata Rao Peta, Chendradana, Medakpally, Ippapahad, Kuppagandla, Velugommula, Vadyal, Madharam, Mokkurala, Gundur, Macharla, Jillella, Veljal, Rachalapally, etc. He was instrumental in founding MB Congregations in several other villages. He baptised over 500 people and solemnised over 225 marriages.

Zachariah had a gospel team with Rev. G.C. Krupaiah (Pastor of MB Church Akuthotapally village) and Rev. M.P. John (Pastor of MB Church, Veldanda village). They are known as the 'Kalwakurthy Trio,' who toured several villages with the gospel of Jesus Christ. Folk Art was one of the effective methods they used to present Bible stories and the gospel. They were folk artists. The trio was outstanding for *Burrakatha,* a Telugu folk. The trio used to narrate 'The Birth of Jesus' and 'The Story of David' in *Burrakatha* to spread the good news of Jesus in the villages. As a result, it is believed that the 'Kalwakurthy Trio' won over 5000 souls for Christ.

Moreover, he was vital in establishing a mission hospital, school, and hostel in Kalwakurthy. He served as the school's correspondent and hostel warden in the 1970s.

Zachariah held different positions at the field and conference levels. He served as chairman and secretary of the MB Field Association, Kalwakurthy, for many years. He also worked as director of MB Property Association Pvt. Ltd., vice-chairman of Committee of Reference and Counsel (CRC), member-GC, chairman-Convention Committee, etc. As a peacemaker, Zachariah played a significant role in solving problems among the MB Churches.

Conclusion

The preceding pages explored the effects of the work of local workers on the emergence, growth, and development of the Mennonite Brethren Church of India. Besides evangelism and church planting, local workers also significantly taught the poor and Dalits. Local workers motivated many parents to send their children to mission or village schools.

Local workers encouraged new social understandings in the informal settings in which they participated. Accordingly, many among the poor, the marginalized, and the downtrodden were trained in higher education through the MB mission's generous programmes. Local workers served as teachers and principals in mission schools. They played a significant role in upgrading schools. Moreover, local workers encouraged young people to pursue theological education, thus encouraging them to become agents of change and channels of grace in the larger society.

MB believers have held some of the highest positions in the government and private sectors. Hence, the MB church significantly uplifts the Telangana region, especially in medical services, education, and even politics.

Despite the hostility of many upper caste people or others, local workers boldly continued their work. Memories of Local workers' sacrificial work remain in people's hearts. To God be the glory for the life and ministry of local workers!

However, during the course of time, MB clinics, hospitals, schools, village schools, etc., that played a significant role in empowering the poor, Dalits, and women today have disappeared. Hence, the need of the hour is to empower local churches with 'Renewal Impulses' that will lead to new solidarity and a stronger sense of peace witness. The church needs to be an agent of peace in a larger society.

Bibliography

"A Brief History of Rev. M.J. Krupaiah in his own words as told to Mr. O. Pavithra Sagar." Printed Pamphlet, Shamshabad, August 2020.

Abraham, P.V. "Sevaku devuni yokka pilupu." [God's call to ministry]. Manuscript, 18 April 1988, Irvin, Kalwakurthy.

Agustin, P. "Late. Rev. V. Isaac Pastor Gaari Sakshyam." [Testimony of Late. Rev. V. Isaac pastor]. Devarakonda: MB Church Thawklapuram, 2016.

Anandam, G.C. "Sakshyam." [Testimony]. A Printed Document, Nagarukurnool, n.d.

Arnold, P.B. "Gollapally Panthulu and Panthulamma." Typed Script, Shamshabad, January 2021.

Asheervadam, K. "Tributes: Celebrating the Life of Rev. E.M. Samuel." Gafoornagar, 9 December 2014.

Augustine, Pachigolla. "Thawklapuram Bethaniya M.B. church charithra" [History of Bethaniya M.B. church Thawklapuram]. Devarakonda: MB Church Thawklapuram, 2016.

Beracah MB Church, *Beracah MB sangha charithra Shabad mariyu Ki.She. K.E. Paul gaari charithra. Vajrothsava vedukalu* (Telugu). Shabad: Beracah MB Church, 2011.

Brief Statement to the American Mennonite Brethren Mission Missionary Council, Shamshabad December 1958. Report of Legal Papers, Documents Pertaining To: Conference of the Mennonite Brethren Church of North America, American Mennonite Brethren Mission, Governing Council of the Conference of the Mennonite Brethren Church in India. Mahabubnagar. 23 December 1958.

Dalavai, Arthur J. *The Tallest Tree in the IMB Field: The History of Dr. Rev. M.B. John.* n.p.: Son and Daughters of Dr. Rev. M.B. John, 2003.

David, A.S. "Brief Biography of Late A.S. Caleb." (Telugu) Manuscript, Shamshabad, 2001.

Foreign Missions in India. The AMBM in India 1898-1948. Hillsboro: Board of Foreign Missions of the Conference of the MBC North America, 1948.

Hardway, Gary. "India Women's Leader, 31. Dies in Vehicle Accident." *Mennonite Weekly Review* (1 August 1996).

Jayaker, Yennamalla. "Biography of Rev. Y.R. Devadanam (1945-2012)." Hyderabad, 27 March, 2012.

______. "Mennonite Brethren Church of India: Transforming Conflict." *The Conrad Grebel Review* 35/3 (Fall 2017): 388-390.

______. "Mennonite Brethren Missionary Women Encounter with Dalit Women in Colonial South India." Paper presented at the Academic Conference on 'Crossing the Line: Women of Anabaptist Traditions Encounter Borders and Boundaries,' at Eastern Mennonite University, Harrisonburg, Virginia, USA, 22-25 June 2017.

______. "Mennonite Brethren Mission in India Then and Now: The Need for Ongoing Renewal." Paper

Presented at an International Colloquium on 'Renewal Movements and Anabaptist History,' Bienenberg, Liestal, Switzerland, 28 March 2019.

________. "Mennonite Brethren Mission and Social Change in South Telangana from 1899-1958: A Subaltern Reading." D.Th., dissertation, Senate of Serampore College (University), 2019.

________. "Mennonites as Agents for Peacebuilding in India." Paper Presented at 'Global Mennonite Peacebuilding Conference and Festival,' Conrad Grebel University College, Waterloo, Ontario, Canada, 11 June 2016.

________. "Obituary: Life and Legacy of Rev. Y. Kamalamma Devadanam (1948-2021)." Hyderabad, 14 April 2021.

________. "Obituary of Rev. R. Praveen Kumar (1973-2021)." Printed Script, Shamshabad, 13 May 2021.

________. "Rev. N.P. James: The First National Principal of MB Bible School Shamshabad." Paper Presented at MBCBC, Shamshabad, 30 January 2018.

________. "Rev. P.V. Abraham gaari jeevitham, paricharya (1901-1991)." [life and ministry of Rev. P.V. Abraham]. Manuscript, 27 September 2021.

________. "The Role of the Mennonite Brethren Church of India in the Upliftment of Telangana Society from 1958-2008." M.Th. Thesis, Senate of Serampore College (University), 2011.

________. "The State of MB Archives in India." Paper Presented at an International Symposium on 'Power and Preservation: Enabling Access to the Sources Behind Our Stories,' Goshen College, Goshen, Indiana, USA, 17-19 June 2019.

Jayaker, Y.D. "Mennonite Brethren Church of India Contribution to Nation Building." *Indian Theological*

Journal 8/1 & 2 (2014): 90-107.

Kaufman, Edmund George. *The Development of the Missionary and Philanthropic Interest among the Mennonites of North America*. Indiana: The Mennonite Book Concern, 1931.

Lazarus, B. "Suvarthannu Paadina Sundaramma." Suvarthamani 69/8 (August 1992): 33.

Lohrenz, J.H. *The Mennonite Brethren Church*. Kanas: The M.B. Publishing House, 1950.

Marthi, Tejaswi. "Keeping Burra Katha Alive in the Wave of Impersonal Storytelling Art Forms." *The Hindu* (Vijayawada), 19 August 2019.

Mathews David, Nanem. "Shraddhanjali." Printed Pamphlet, Balapur, Ranga Reddy district, 2020.

M.B. Mission Centenary Celebrations Nagarkurnool (1904-2004) Souvenir. Nagarkurnool: MB Church, 2004.

Memorandum and Articles of Association of Mennonite Brethren Property Association of India Private Limited, 1974.

Menon, V.P. *Integration of the Indian States*. Rev. ed. Hyderabad: Orient BlackSwan [1956], 2014.

Narimalla, Vidya. "Abel P. Ballem (1907–1999): Invited into God's Story." *Profiles of Mennonite Faith* 51 (Winter 2012).

Penner, Peter. *Russians, North Americans and Telugus: The Mennonite Brethren Mission in India, 1885-1975*. Hillsboro: CMBS, 1997.

Purushotham, D.N., comp. *Mennonite Brethren Theological Graduates with Their Life History and Literary Contributions*. Hyderabad: G.J. Douglas, 2012.

Ramulu, B.S. *Telangana State Need of Revival*. Hyderabad: University of Social Philosophy, 2008.

Solomon, E.D., comp. "60 Samvathsaraala devuni krupalo Rev. V. K. Rufus (1942 -)." [60 Years of God's Grace Rev. V. K. Rufus (1942 -)]. Shamshabad:

MBCBC & BMBC, 2003.

Sundarayya, P. *Telangana People's Struggle and its Lessons.* Hyderabad: Foundation Books, 2006.

Toews, John A. *A History of the Mennonite Brethren Church: Pilgrims and Pioneers.* Fresno: BCLGCMC, 1975.

Wiebe, Paul D. and David A. Wiebe. *In Another Day of the Lord.* Winnipeg: Kindred Productions, 2010.

Wiebe, Paul D. *Christians in Andhra Pradesh: The Mennonites of Mahbubnagar.* Madras: CLS, 1988.

__________. *Heirs and Joint Heirs. Mission to Church among the Mennonite Brethren of Andhra Pradesh.* Winnipeg: Kindred Productions, 2010.

Interviews

Arnold, P.B. Son of Pastor Benjamin Perumalla, Shamshabad. Interview, 29 October 2020.

Augustine, Pachigolla. Pastor Thawklapuram. Interview, 12 February 2018.

Daniel, A.C. Son of A.S. Caleb and Journalist, Shamshabad. Interview, 20 January 2021.

David, C.A. Secretary of MB Church, Achampeta. Interview, 23 November 2020.

David, J.L. Executive Director of MBDO, Jadcherla. Interview, 28 December 2020.

David, P.A. Second son of Pastor P.V. Abraham, Hyderabad. Interview, 20 December 2020.

Dayaker, Y.D. Vice-chairman of Faith MB Church, Chandrayan Gutta, Hyd. Interview, 10 April 2021.

Dorothy Bhaskar, G. Wife of G.Y. Bhaskar, Shamshabad. Interview, 2 September 2021.

Emmanuel, G.A. Eldest son of Rev. G.C. Anandam, Mahabubnagar. Interview, 20 February 2021.

Joseph, E.S. Eldest son of Rev. E.M. Samuel, Shamshabad. Interview on the phone, 9 July 2020.

Joseph, S.J. Director of Christian Concern Mission, Shamshabad. Interview, 25 September 2021

Kamalamma, Y.D. Wife of Rev. Y.R. Devadanam, Hyderabad. Interview, 18 February 2021.

Krupaiah, M.J. Advisor of the MB Field Association Shamshabad. Interview, 14 March 2017.

Lemuel, B.L. Pastor and Chairman of MB Church Penjarla. Interview, 20 May 2021.

Padma, G.P. Chairman of the Bethany MB Women Fellowship, Shamshabad. Interview, 2 October 2021.

Praveen, R.D. Son of G.J. Prabhavathi Devapriyam, Shamshabad. Interview, 30 September 2021.

Premalatha, G.V. Wife of G.Y. Vidyasagar, Shamshabad. Interview, 30 September 2021.

Purushotham, K.V. Treasurer - GC, Nagarkurnool. Interview, 4 March 2021.

Purushotham, M.J. Pastor MB Church Neelam Nagar, Mallepally. Interview, 14 September 2021.

Samuel Prasad, S. Pastor of Bethany MB Church, Shamshabad. Interview, 10 September 2020.

Sharamma, K.S. Younger sister of Rev. E.M. Samuel, Shadnagar. Interview, 9 July 2020.

Talwar, David. Pastor - MB Field Narayanpet. Interview, 30 June 2021.

Timothy, K.B. Son of Rev. K.R. Benjamin. Interview on the phone, 19 May 2021.

Timothy, R.P. Son of Rev. R. Praveen Kumar. Interview on the phone, 23 May 2021.

Vedulla, Dennis. Younger son of Rev. V.K. Rufus, Shamshabad. Interview, 18 October 2018.